WOMEN, POWER AND POLITICS

THEN

THE MILLINER AND THE WEAVER
Marie Jones

THE LIONESS
Rebecca Lenkiewicz

HANDBAGGED
Moira Buffini

BLOODY WIMMIN
Lucy Kirkwood

Also available in a companion volume:

NOW

ACTING LEADER by Joy Wilkinson
THE PANEL by Zinnie Harris
PLAYING THE GAME by Bola Agbaje
PINK by Sam Holcroft
YOU, ME AND Wii by Sue Townsend

D1384820

Other Titles by Nick Hern Books

Jez Butterworth
JERUSALEM
MOJO
THE NIGHT HERON
PARLOUR SONG
THE WINTERLING

Caryl Churchill
BLUE HEART
CHURCHILL PLAYS: THREE
CHURCHILL PLAYS: FOUR
CHURCHILL: SHORTS
CLOUD NINE
A DREAM PLAY *after* Strindberg
DRUNK ENOUGH TO SAY
    I LOVE YOU?
FAR AWAY
HOTEL
ICECREAM
LIGHT SHINING IN
    BUCKINGHAMSHIRE
MAD FOREST
A NUMBER
SEVEN JEWISH CHILDREN
THE SKRIKER
THIS IS A CHAIR
THYESTES *after* Seneca
TRAPS

Helen Edmundson
ANNA KARENINA *after* Tolstoy
THE CLEARING
CORAM BOY *after* Gavin
GONE TO EARTH *after* Webb
LIFE IS A DREAM *after* Calderón
MILL ON THE FLOSS *after* Eliot
MOTHER TERESA IS DEAD
ORESTES
WAR AND PEACE *after* Tolstoy

Stella Feehily
DREAMS OF VIOLENCE
DUCK
O GO MY MAN

debbie tucker green
BORN BAD
DIRTY BUTTERFLY
RANDOM
STONING MARY
TRADE & GENERATIONS

Sam Holcroft
COCKROACH

Lucy Kirkwood
HEDDA *after* Ibsen
IT FELT EMPTY WHEN THE
    HEART WENT AT FIRST BUT
    IT IS ALRIGHT NOW
TINDERBOX

Liz Lochhead
BLOOD AND ICE
DRACULA *after* Bram Stoker
EDUCATING AGNES ('The School
    for Wives') *after* Molière
GOOD THINGS
MARY QUEEN OF SCOTS GOT
    HER HEAD CHOPPED OFF
MEDEA *after* Euripides
MISERYGUTS & TARTUFFE
    after Molière
PERFECT DAYS
THEBANS

Marie Jones
NIGHT IN NOVEMBER &
    STONES IN HIS POCKETS

Conor McPherson
DUBLIN CAROL
McPHERSON: FOUR PLAYS
McPHERSON PLAYS: TWO
PORT AUTHORITY
THE SEAFARER
SHINING CITY
THE WEIR

Chloë Moss
CHRISTMAS IS MILES AWAY
HOW LOVE IS SPELT
THIS WIDE NIGHT
THE WAY HOME

ELAINE MURPHY
Little Gem

Joanna Murray Smith
BOMBSHELLS
THE FEMALE OF THE SPECIES
HONOUR

Diane Samuels
KINDERTRANSPORT
THREE SISTERS ON HOPE STREET
    with Tracy-Ann Oberman
THE TRUE LIFE FICTION OF
    MATA HARI

Joy Wilkinson
FAIR & FAIR EFFECTS

WOMEN,
POWER AND POLITICS
THEN

MARIE JONES ■ THE MILLINER AND THE WEAVER

REBECCA LENKIEWICZ ■ THE LIONESS

MOIRA BUFFINI ■ HANDBAGGED

LUCY KIRKWOOD ■ BLOODY WIMMIN

Introduced by Indhu Rubasingham

NICK HERN BOOKS
London
www.nickhernbooks.co.uk

A Nick Hern Book

Women, Power and Politics: Then first published in Great Britain in 2010 as a paperback original by Nick Hern Books Limited, 14 Larden Road, London W3 7ST, in association with the Tricycle Theatre, London

The Milliner and the Weaver copyright © 2010 Marie Jones
The Lioness copyright © 2010 Rebecca Lenkiewicz
Handbagged copyright © 2010 Moira Buffini
Bloody Wimmin copyright © 2010 Lucy Kirkwood
Introduction copyright © 2010 Indhu Rubasingham

The authors have asserted their moral rights

Cover designed by Ned Hoste, 2H
Cover image by feastcreative.com

Typeset by Nick Hern Books, London
Printed and bound in Great Britain by by CLE Print Ltd, St Ives, Cambs PE27 3LE

A CIP catalogue record for this book is available from the British Library

ISBN 978 1 84842 116 5

Contents

Introduction
Indhu Rubasingham

Women, Power and Politics is a season of nine exciting new plays presented in two parts, *Then* and *Now*. Creating it has been an important journey where theatre is reflecting, amongst other things, the immediate politics of today. This journey started a year ago.

In May 2009 the Tricycle had just opened *The Great Game: Afghanistan*. I co-directed it with Nick Kent, who produced the project at the Tricycle in North London, where he is the Artistic Director. It was a day-long event featuring a series of twelve new plays looking at Afghan history from the first Anglo-Afghan War up to the present day. It was proving to be a huge success and a very special production. Two days after the press 'day', whilst I was lying in a darkened room recovering from this enormous endeavour, Nick called me to say that he had a great idea he wanted to discuss. I was amazed by his unstoppable energy. He had just read an article in *The Times* where there was a picture of David Cameron presiding over the then Shadow Cabinet, which consisted entirely of (white) men. The article was discussing where the women were in the Tory Party. Inspired by this, Nick offered me the opportunity to direct and produce a project looking at and titled *Women, Power and Politics* on a similar template to *The Great Game*.

It was a unique opportunity to conceive and produce a project on this scale. Where do you start? To begin with I thought about international politics, working with writers from all over the world. However, as I started to research, I soon realised that given it was such a broad subject, if I went too wide I would only be able to skim the surface. I was going to have to narrow it down – and soon. But the statistics internationally were fascinating and the issues complex. How do you define politics and power? The canvas felt very, very big and, at times, daunting. It is, moreover, a subject which raises such passion in people.

Opinions, both varied and extreme, were offered on what material the plays should contain. Unlike *The Great Game*, where the majority of people in this country were fairly unaware of the situation in Afghanistan, everyone is aware of this subject and holds a fervent opinion on it: whether it is Margaret Thatcher or the expenses scandal surrounding Jacqui Smith and her husband. It was also interesting how different generations had very different perspectives and agendas.

The fog slowly lifted and, after much discussion with my team (more about them soon), I decided that the theatre was going to be specific to women, power and politics in Great Britain; while the Tricycle's cinema would look at women in politics internationally; and its gallery would offer a celebration of women in Great Britain. It was also important to me that the programme would create debate and discussion amongst the audience and be of the highest artistic quality. Theatre is a fantastic medium for emotional engagement, and it is something we experience as a collective; I wanted the event to demonstrate the complexity of issues that should concern and engage everybody. In the theatre, we are not there to define answers but to provoke questions.

At the time of writing, we have just had a General Election. Women make up 22% of Parliament. There are only four women in the new Cabinet which works out at less than 20% and far less than most other Western democracies. Spain, Germany, France, Sweden, Norway, Italy, Greece, the USA and Belgium are just a few of the countries that have a much higher percentage of women in Government and in the Cabinet. Yet women make up 52% of the population of the UK. During the election campaign of 2010, it was the wives of the party leaders who had far more media coverage than any female politician or candidate. This new era of British politics is especially worrying as there seems to be little or no interest or concern about the lack of representation. This is ironic considering the fanfare surrounding 'Blair's Babes' in 1997. Why is this happening and what are the obstacles that are preventing women from entering or gaining power within the political system in this country? Is it the structure of government? The media? Society? Or is it women themselves?

I created a small team who would meet regularly to bounce ideas and discuss the project. This included Zoe Ingenhaag, Ruth Needham, Holly Conneely and Rachel Taylor. This team sometimes expanded to engage more voices, but on the whole this was the core group. Different generations of women discussing and tussling over this material was thrilling and thought-provoking. One example will serve for many: it became apparent that the two younger ones had never heard of Greenham Common and were unaware of such an enormous political event in the 1980s. This was suprising and led us to asking: why had this event been lost to a younger generation, and what is its legacy?

There were going to be two parts to this project, each containing four or five plays. The two parts would be played alternately on weekday evenings, and together on Saturdays. The first part would look at historical issues and the second part would look at the current situation. This was primarily decided in order to give the two parts a distinctive quality. Nick Kent suggested introducing a verbatim element, for which the Tricycle is renowned, and introduced me to Gillian Slovo. We met and decided that she would interview a variety of politicians and then edit the pieces to form a backbone to the whole event. They would be interspersed between the plays and give us the current reality of women politicians.

After the groundwork had been done, I started to approach playwrights, some I knew and others I did not. I went to Belfast and met Marie Jones; persuaded Zinnie Harris who was pregnant and already overly busy; commissioned old colleagues and friends with whom I hadn't worked but long admired: Moira Buffini and Rebecca Lenkiewicz, and young writers whose energy, skill and voice really impressed and excited me like Lucy Kirkwood, Sam Holcroft and Joy Wilkinson. I had just worked with Bola Agbaje on her play, *Detaining Justice*, and really wanted her perspective and zest; when Sue Townsend was interested, well, what can I say: I grew up on her writing.

I met and talked with each writer about the entire concept. Most of them chose subjects and topics that they were interested in, others I suggested ideas to, but all these playwrights were enthusiastic and passionate about the subject.

I made sure that the content of the plays did not overlap and waited impatiently for the first drafts. The National Theatre Studio very kindly hosted the project for a week in order to develop the scripts with actors. This proved invaluable for the development process.

The plays are incredibly exciting. The content, form and voice are unique in each play, and yet each packs a punch and is complex in its ideas. Viewing them alongside each other in production is bound to produce a stimulating and intense evening. It is an honour to be working with so much talent and I am grateful to the playwrights for their wonderful plays.

I have to thank Mel Kenyon for her advice and support, as well as Jack Bradley. Purni Morell and the National Theatre Studio have been very generous. It is a privilege to be working with Rosa Maggiora and Amy Hodge on this production with an incredibly talented and brilliant company of actors. None of this would have happened without my core team, and Zoe Ingenhaag has been the rock of this project. Finally, none of this would even be taking place if it were not for Nick Kent and his team at the Tricycle.

May 2010

Then was first performed at the Tricycle Theatre, London, as part of the *Women, Power and Politics* season on 4 June 2010, with the following casts:

THE MILLINER AND THE WEAVER

HENRIETTA	Niamh Cusack
ELSPETH	Stella Gonet
THOMAS	Felix Scott

THE LIONESS

QUEEN ELIZABETH I	Niamh Cusack
NEUZER	Simon Chandler
JOHN KNOX	Tom Mannion
ESSEX	Oliver Chris
COURTIERS	John Hollingworth
	Felix Scott

HANDBAGGED

T	Stella Gonet
Q	Kika Markham
MAGS	Heather Craney
LIZ	Claire Cox
RON	Tom Mannion
SHEA	Simon Chandler

BLOODY WIMMIN

HELEN	Claire Cox
LITTLE GIRL /	
HANNAH / LIV	Amy Loughton
REPORTER / LOU	Heather Craney
GRAHAM	Felix Scott
MARGARET	Niamh Cusack
LORRAINE	Stella Gonet
BOB	Oliver Chris
JACK	Simon Chandler
DAN	Tom Mannion
JAMES	John Hollingworth
SOPHIE	Lara Rossi
LILLIAN	Kika Markham

Director	Indhu Rubasingham
Designer	Rosa Maggiora
Lighting Designer	Matt Eagland
Sound Designer	Tom Lishman
Associate Director	Amy Hodge
Associate Producer	Zoe Ingenhaag
Dramaturg	Rachel Taylor

This text went to press before the end of rehearsals and so may differ slightly from the plays as performed.

THE MILLINER AND THE WEAVER

Marie Jones

Marie Jones is an award-winning Irish writer and has written extensively for stage and television. *Stones in His Pocket*s was an international success and won the Olivier Award for Best Comedy, the Evening Standard Award for Best Comedy and the Irish Times/ESB Best Production Award. The show has been produced on the West End and Broadway and in over thirty countries worldwide. Two of her other works, *Women on the Verge of HRT* and *A Night in November,* were sell-out shows in the West End and Broadway. They were revived in London and Belfast in 2008, and *HRT* toured the UK in 2009 starring Sarah Lancashire.

Marie is one of the founding members of the Charabanc Theatre Company and was its Writer-in-Residence from 1983–90. She also works as an actress, playing Sarah Conlon in the Jim Sheridan film, *In the Name of the Father*. Marie received the John Hewitt Award for outstanding contribution to culture, tradition and the arts in Northern Ireland. She has also been awarded two Honorary Doctorates from Queens University and University of Ulster, and is an OBE.

Characters

HENRIETTA GIRVAN, *from Belfast, a widowed mill worker,
a weaver, in her early forties*
ELSPETH SMITH, *from Dublin, wife of a Dublin businessman,
late thirties*
THOMAS GIRVAN, *son of Henrietta, sixteen*

Belfast, 1914.

The play is set in the small mill house in East Belfast, the home of HENRIETTA *and her six children.*

The house does not have much: a chest, a few chairs, a sideboard and a scrubbed table. On the sideboard are a few cups, a teapot, milk and sugar.

Somewhere upstage a window looking onto the street.

In a blackout we hear distant marching and a crowd cheering... and occasionally a voice... 'Left left, left right left.'

Lights up onstage.

HENRIETTA *stands in front of the scrubbed table... she is washing socks in a tin basin and hanging them individually on a line... underneath the table there are four sets of dirty shoes or boots. She stops and goes to the window to listen to the marching... goes back to the basin and the scrubbing.*

A knock at her door... she stops... does not move... we can see she is concerned... again the door knocks.

She goes to the door.

HENRIETTA. Elspeth... In the name a God, what are you doin' up here?

HENRIETTA *pulls her into the house.*

ELSPETH. Is it a bad time?

HENRIETTA. It's just... I'm just... well, as you can see.

ELSPETH *is well dressed in a beautiful expensive hat, she looks incongruous to the surroundings.* HENRIETTA *is embarrassed by this.*

ELSPETH. Sorry... yes... yes... I see you're busy... I won't stay long.

As HENRIETTA *speaks, she goes to the door and locks it from the inside. She is uncomfortable and does not want to look* ELSPETH *in the eye.*

HENRIETTA. You come all this way… to see me.

ELSPETH. Yes, well no, I did have a meeting in the Belfast office… spent most of the time brushing up… windows broken again.

HENRIETTA. Aye… socks and shoes… the bane of m'life… I dream about them… all marchin' towards me, a big army of stinkin' socks and shoes… all defiant buggers marchin' at me… and just as they get this close they stop and wait… wait for me to feel sorry for them and gather them all up and wash and clean them and make them better, but you know what I want to do… grab them and dump the whole bloody lot in the Lagan, watch them splutterin' their way intil the Irish Sea and away for ever… then laugh m'head off.

ELSPETH. Henrietta, are you alright?

HENRIETTA. NO… no, I'm not… It was the knock at the door, it put the heart across me.

ELSPETH. I didn't mean to alarm…

HENRIETTA. It's alright, you're not to know… m'door is always on the latch… if a door knocks round here, it's trouble… a debt man, or worse, a poor-law guardian… thank God I have been managing, but you never know, they could send them for spite to take us to the poorhouse.

ELSPETH. Why did you lock the door?

HENRIETTA. What.

ELSPETH. Just now.

HENRIETTA. It's dark.

ELSPETH. You said it's always open.

HENRIETTA. I'm feared.

ELSPETH. Sorry, if I had known me being here would cause you trouble.

HENRIETTA. I'm not feared for me… I'm feared for you… they're not used to strangers comin' here unless it's trouble. Did you speak to anybody in the street?

ELSPETH. No.

HENRIETTA. You think anybody seen you?

ELSPETH. I don't know who saw me, I didn't think to notice, I spoke to nobody… the street seemed deserted.

HENRIETTA. Aye. All up the next street cheerin' the men… they'll be marchin' down here… did you pass them on your way?

ELSPETH. I could hear them.

HENRIETTA. You'll see them soon.

She carries on vigorously scrubbing the socks. Nobody speaks… it is still uncomfortable.

God knows what the neighbours will be thinking.

ELSPETH. I don't care what they think, I came to see you.

HENRIETTA. I bloody care, it's me that lives here… anyhow, it's too late now, somebody will know you're here… they have eyes in their arses in this street… you should have thought, you read the papers… how did you find me?

ELSPETH. When you stopped coming to the meetings… I checked the registry for your address.

HENRIETTA. There's others stopped, why me?

ELSPETH. There weren't many like you.

HENRIETTA. None with a gob on them like me… not like the fancy dames with fancy words.

ELSPETH. Like me, you mean?

HENRIETTA *says nothing*.

No… You're right.

HENRIETTA. It's important, you know, clean shoes and socks… everything else you can get by without scrubbin' for a day or two… but not the feet… they check them, the teachers, you're a bad mother if they aren't clean… if you're stayin', say what you came to say.

ELSPETH. This damned Home Rule business.

HENRIETTA. The tea in that pot will still be warm, there's milk and sugar and a cup on the sideboard.

ELSPETH. You're sure.

HENRIETTA. It's only a cup a tea, my mother always reared us to offer, even if we didn't mean it.

A pause… ELSPETH *is not sure if she does mean it*.

You want me to make it for you.

ELSPETH. No… tea… that would be nice… thank you.

HENRIETTA. Well…? I am sure you haven't come all this road just to tell me something I already know.

ELSPETH. No… I wanted you to know how much you meant to us… how brave… what a loss you are.

HENRIETTA. To change my mind, talk me into going back.

ELSPETH. I didn't come to change anybody's mind.

HENRIETTA. Never stopped you before.

ELSPETH. Nor you.

HENRIETTA. It's different now. I have to keep my head down and say nothin'… understand? The women don't want to know now… even Mrs Pankhurst, for all her great speechifying… there's not a woman round here would listen… not now… you lost their trust.

ELSPETH. We can't let this take away from all that we've done... I wanted you to know that... you had... still have so much to give.

HENRIETTA. I thought we could make things better.

ELSPETH. We can.

HENRIETTA. Maybe you can.

ELSPETH. The women were listening to you...

HENRIETTA. The women who stood with me and cheered you that first day when you spoke outside the mill. They had never heard talk like that. I seen the change in them after that, they wanted me to speak up for them... Etti, we won't be walked over no more, you tell them that, Etti. They wanted to walk out on strike if they didn't get what was proper... a strike here in a Belfast mill, could you imagine that... I spoke, but it was their voice.

ELSPETH. Exactly.

HENRIETTA. Then it all changed.

ELSPETH. But nothing has changed for them... their lives are still the same.

HENRIETTA. Those same women are now abusing me in the street... 'Fenien lover'. After all that hard work. They accused me of siding with them that want to destroy the Protestant people, that's all that matters now... we have no support round here no more... there is no point... I wouldn't even be surprised that those same women, whose lives you think you can change, chucked the bricks that broke your office windows.

ELSPETH. No matter, the organisation will still support them, their rights... you can speak to them, tell them.

HENRIETTA. What organisation... laughable now... split into that many groups... Catholics, Protestants, Northerners, Southerners, Christians, Heathens... can't keep up, there's that many... and you call that organisation... spare me.

ELSPETH. That's because most of them have lost sight of the most important thing, what was keeping us together... now they don't see further than their own damned back yards... it's bloody infuriating.

HENRIETTA. That damned back yard is where they live their lives... ya think any of the women round here care if they ever go to university or get into Parliament... half a them can't even read or write, for Christ's sake... It's over... it's too late...

The sounds of marching and cheering getting close.

ELSPETH *is uncomfortable.*

It's fine... the door is locked. Look.

They go to the window.

The sounds of men marching past the window and people cheering.

Look... man and boy prepared to fight and save Ulster... save it from their own countrymen, young men, my son... look, all fired up, proud... and so bloody blind... scary... so terrible scary.

HENRIETTA *goes to the chest and brings out a pair of boots to clean.*

Our Isaac's... look at the state of them. The only way I could stop him from runnin' out there and joining in was to hide his boots. He went to bed cryin' and sceamin' that he wanted to march with the volunteers like his brother. He is twelve years old, for God's sake... a child, what does he know... I know someday soon he will just follow like the rest; I won't be able to stop that... did you see fear on those men's faces, did you?

ELSPETH. No... no, I didn't.

HENRIETTA. Pride, pride and ignorance, is what I see... it's me that has the fear... they'll march on and on, they'll only know fear when they come face to face with death itself... then it's too late.

Oh Christ, I could scream... you shouldn't have made that bloody speech.

HENRIETTA *slams the boot on the table... and starts to polish vigourously.*

I wanted to stop you, pull you off that platform... standin' there all puffed up and clever, telling these women they stand a better chance if Ireland has Home Rule.

ELSPETH. It's what I believe.

HENRIETTA. And did you think you would get cheers from the crowds... were you bloody stupid?

ELSPETH. Not everyone is going to like what I say...

HENRIETTA. Well, you certainly got that right.

ELSPETH. Well, I am not sorry that what I feel is not what you want to hear.

HENRIETTA. I didn't say I didn't want to hear it, and whether I agree with you or not, it's not about me, it's about... all this, this place, all of it, every brick, every cobble, it's ingrained... that's when I knew I couldn't go back... couldn't associate.

ELSPETH. I still believe what I said.

HENRIETTA. Sometimes it's better to keep things to yourself, until the time is right.

ELSPETH. The one thing we were all fightin' for... where is that... do they even remember now?

HENRIETTA. Face it, Elspeth... we are just all the bits of a smashed plate... Lord Carson and Mr Asquith can rub their hands in glee... they broke us and they didn't even have to get out of their beds to do it, we did it ourselves.

ELSPETH. Look... look at this.

ELSPETH *brings a newspaper out of her bag.*

Henrietta, look... It's the *New York Times*... we were reported in the *New York Times*, Henrietta, we reached America.

HENRIETTA. America.

ELSPETH. Listen to this headline. 'Tumult in Belfast Court.'

HENRIETTA. A what?

ELSPETH. Tumult… like a commotion and uproar.

HENRIETTA. Like a tumour in your head… was it that bad?

ELSPETH. Yes.

HENRIETTA. Good.

ELSPETH. The first time ever in a Belfast court.

HENRIETTA. That wait for your signal, remember.

ELSPETH. I nearly didn't do it… the fear of what could happen to all of us.

HENRIETTA. I would never have forgive you if you hadn't… I never knew a feeling like that, all us women doing something together… when we started roarin' and shoutin', I was beside myself… I couldn't stop… didn't want to stop.

ELSPETH. You said to me, 'I hope we will be remembered for this, if nothing else, we did this…' Well, we were… (*Reads.*) 'Judges dodge missiles.'

HENRIETTA. Missiles… it was a bag a brandy balls and a grip bag.

ELSPETH. 'Judges dodge brandy balls'? This is the *New York Times*.

HENRIETTA. Well, excuse me.

ELSPETH. You see what we've done.

HENRIETTA (*a smile*). Me a weaver, dressed like a toff in your hat and coat.

ELSPETH (*reads*). 'The Suffragettes kept up the uproar until forty of them were ejected from the courts, but the noise still continued and the magistrate finally decided to suspend the sitting. As the two female prisoners were led out, they shrieked.'

HENRIETTA. 'Shrieked'…? What cheeky bugger wrote that…
they didn't bloody shriek, that's what weeins do… they
shouted loud and clear. 'We will not permit the holding of a
court that doesn't recognise our civil rights.'

ELSPETH. Yes, remember that, Henrietta, always remember that.

HENRIETTA. You have a family, Elspeth?

ELSPETH. I have a husband… yes.

HENRIETTA. Does he support you doin' all this?

ELSPETH. He has more interest in what's on his dinner plate
than a woman with a vote.

HENRIETTA. What about the movement, he knows about that.

ELSPETH. Oh absolutely, 'I'm proud of you, Essy, for standing
up for what is only just and proper.'

HENRIETTA. That's good.

ELSPETH (*mimics him*). 'Other men would have no time for
their wives behaving in such an unfeminine manner, but not
me, Essy, I'm a man ahead of my time.'

HENRIETTA. Cheek.

ELSPETH. Oh, I let him ramble on.

HENRIETTA. At least he supports you, that's half the battle,
isn't it.

ELSPETH. If you could call it that… last week he came barging
into the kitchen waving his newspaper… outraged… 'Good
God, Essy, have you read this… it's preposterous… women
breaking windows, burning postboxes, behaving like
savages… ruining any chance now of getting a vote, and
humiliating their own race into the bargain.'

HENRIETTA. But you, you were part of all that.

ELSPETH. Eight of us were arrested… I can't get arrested…
God, no… sometimes when I have to listen to his pompous
ramblings about how he supports me… I want to smother

him with a pillow so I never have to hear it again. My husband and I are known in certain circles in Dublin... so I have an old mill apron and shawl.

HENRIETTA. You go out lookin' like me?

ELSPETH. I'm sorry, I didn't mean... I don't mean that I...

HENRIETTA. It's alright, didn't I have to go to the court looking like you... I think I got the better costume, though.

ELSPETH. We heard a rumour one day that Asquith was trying to pay a secret visit to Dublin and he was at dinner in the Gresham Hotel... so a crowd of us gathered outside to wait for him, placards, chantin', the usual... naturally the police arrived to move us on, naturally we took to giving them abuse... then I saw him, my husband coming up the street towards us, I knew I couldn't run, wouldn't leave the other women... this is it, I thought... he stopped, looked at us and right at me, he said, right into my face... 'You damned women are your own worst enemy, God help the poor men you are married to.'

HENRIETTA. He didn't recognise you... Jesus.

ELSPETH. Then, the worst... he stood there encouraging the police to move us on. One woman chained herself to the hitching post outside the hotel... the police just uprooted the post and carried her off, still chained to it... not one of our better ideas... my husband and others, men and women, cheered as she was carried off... I wanted to kill him... run after him, and let him see that it was me, his wife.

HENRIETTA. Then what?

ELSPETH. I don't know... I would be free of him, the double life, but I am not that strong... yet.

HENRIETTA. Funny, of all the times we met at the offices... I'd think, it's alright for the likes of these women who have no bother standing up in front of crowds, having the time and the money to run here and there to meetings and speechify... and yet I knew nothing about any of them, really... Do you work?

ELSPETH. I have a milliner's shop.

HENRIETTA. A hat shop?

ELSPETH. A hat shop, yes.

HENRIETTA. Lorny days, a hat shop, never knowed anybody that owned a hat shop.

ELSPETH. You think that is funny, why?

HENRIETTA. A hat shop?

ELSPETH. I have a little back room we call, 'The War Department', that's where we plan... it's safe, no man is going to come into a ladies' hat shop... and when I am not there, one of the other women will run it... we take turns... maybe someday you...

HENRIETTA. No... no, that won't happen, but I can see it, you surrounded by all them fancy hats.

ELSPETH. The good thing is my husband wouldn't dare to come in, 'All those ladies, wittering on endlessly about peacock feathers and silk trimmings,' little does he know we're usually planning burning down banks and post offices or kidnapping the Prime Minister.

HENRIETTA. A woman in the street the other day shouted at me... 'Etti Girvan, you're dead lucky you have no man'... lucky? He died of TB and left me to bring up six kids, but I knew what she meant... these women have their men to contend with too.

ELSPETH. Britain has a huge Empire to defend, there will always be wars... I don't want to be part of that, do you?

HENRIETTA. They do, that's what matters now to me... them out there, and they will fight for it... but you're not from here, I don't expect you to understand.

ELSPETH. I'm Irish.

HENRIETTA. This is Ulster, it's different... for better or worse I have to stick with them, it's who I am. Two years ago, almost to the day, we all stood at the docks by the slipway, proud Belfast people… two-hundred thousand men and women, proud of our men who built the biggest ship in the world, the *Titanic*, the unsinkable *Titanic*. That feeling when she slipped away into the water. We didn't have much, any of us on our own, but together we stood proud that our men built that… did that. Two days later and that pride is shattered, thirteen shipyard men from round here went down with her. People here are still mournin'… they refuse to speak of it, you know. There's a dark cloud hangs over this city… you can see it, men that once marched over that Queens Bridge to work on that ship, hard-working men, proud of their work, part of the biggest shipyard in the world, that they made. After that ship went down and fifteen-hundred souls drowned or froze to death… you could see them shuffling over that bridge to work, heads stooped, humiliated, the shame of havin' all that death on their shoulders.

ELSPETH. It was an iceberg.

HENRIETTA. Not how they see it… it was a Roman Catholic curse… that's what ones round here believe… the Catholic curse on the shipyard for not employing them… a curse from the Pope of Rome.

ELSPETH. That is ridiculous…

HENRIETTA. To you, to me, to Mrs Pankhurst… we don't matter… it's what they believe… it's what they want to believe… so over there in London when they decide to bring the Home Rule for Ireland up again… God forgive them, they don't know what they do to this place… they tear it apart.

ELSPETH. Great timing for Sir Edward Carson.

HENRIETTA. Yes, get the Protestants ris up… scare them into believing that everything they have worked for and believe could be taken from them by the same ones that cursed their ship… they will lay down their lives rather than have that.

ELSPETH. Perhaps those people had a reason to curse their ship… maybe it deserved to be cursed… they stopped those

Catholic men from work, took away their dignity, their rights, why would they give a damn about you or your ship.

HENRIETTA. Well, there is the difference between us... you can say that, I can never, even if I believe it... I daren't even think it.

ELSPETH. But we have to face up to it... it will happen again and again... there will be Home Rule, are you always going to just bury your head?

HENRIETTA (*angry*). Don't stand there all jumped up, telling me what I have to face up to... you don't know what I have had to face up to.

ELSPETH. Well then, tell me, tell me, is it any worse than what we have all tried to face... women are being attacked on the streets, in prison on hunger strike.

HENRIETTA. I can't think about those women any more... I have to think about those men who are leading my people and sacrificing them for their own ends... I have to sit here, listen to them give orders to march up and down, preparing to die for Ulster... to take my son and I can say nothin'... That's what I face up to... and it breaks my heart. That first day when I heard you speak in the park about our rights as women, not Catholic or Protestant, but all of us. Now it's about me, and my family, and I don't want to hear any more about anybody else's struggle... no more.

ELSPETH. That's it then, there is no point, I'll go.

As ELSPETH *is about to leave.*

There is a loud banging on the door.

ELSPETH *is frightened, she looks at* HENRIETTA.

The sound of THOMAS'*s voice, off.*

THOMAS (*off*). Ma...! Mammy...! Open the door... are you in there?

HENRIETTA *assures her it's alright.*

HENRIETTA. It's our Thomas.

THOMAS (*more banging*). What's wrong, what's happened, why's our front door locked?

HENRIETTA (*lets him in*). For God's sake… have you left me any door?

THOMAS. What's wrong, Ma, is there trouble?

HENRIETTA. No, son, this is Mrs Elspeth Smith from the WSPU… my eldest, our Thomas.

ELSPETH. Nice to meet you, Thomas.

THOMAS. Oh, so that's why the door was locked… you from Dublin? She's having no more to do with your outfit.

HENRIETTA. Who is *she*… the cat's mother…? And furthermore *she* will speak for herself.

ELSPETH. It's alright, Henrietta.

HENRIETTA. You mind your manners, Thomas Girvan, or you'll feel the back of my hand. Elspeth is a friend of mine, and while she is in my house, she'll get respect… and what has you back to the house, it's not near ten yet.

THOMAS. Quick, Ma, I need our brush.

HENRIETTA. M'brush, what the hell for?

THOMAS. Never mind… my business.

HENRIETTA. And my brush is my business, what do you want it for?

THOMAS. Arms practice.

HENRIETTA. What?

THOMAS. Orders from Sir Edward Carson, the battalion have to practise with brushes.

HENRIETTA. I don't believe it… practise with brushes… practise what with brushes?

THOMAS. Drill… we have to use brushes until we get our real arms.

HENRIETTA. Real arms? What real arms?

THOMAS. God's sake, Ma, it was the talk of the place... two ships from Germany docked last night, full of weapons... there was a whole fleet of lorries and cars with volunteers waitin' to load them. Carson organised it... they're in safe houses all over Ulster.

HENRIETTA. How come you know this?

THOMAS. Our whole battalion knew.

HENRIETTA. Did the police not stop them.

THOMAS. The police? Nah, they just watched, they're loyal Ulster men too... sure, most of them have joined the Ulster Volunteer Force... they have their own battalion. Anyway, here's the laugh, a whole other battalion went down to the Belfast docks and all stood like they were waitin' for this boat called the *Gallemera*. The customs men thought there must be arms on board so they surrounded it... but it was a decoy, cos up at Larne, two boats with the real weapons docked... we have them now, we are ready for the Home Rulers... Carson's army are ready for the fight. You can tell your sort down in Dublin, missus, that Ulster will never be taken from us by no heathen Pope-lovers... and if I were you I would get myself back down there.

HENRIETTA. Shut you up, ya upstart.

ELSPETH. I'm leaving anyway. Thomas, be proud of your mother, she is a very brave woman.

HENRIETTA. Thomas, O – U – T.

THOMAS. My mother is not a traitor, remember that... if I were you I would leave, there is no place for Home Rulers in this street.

HENRIETTA. This is my house and I'll say who comes and goes and what's more, it's my bloody brush too and if Sir Edward Carson wants you to parade up and down pretendin' you're a soldier, tell him to supply ye with a brush, though I doubt he's ever had to use one.

THOMAS. Suit yourself, Ma, but I can tell you this: there will be no shortage of weemin in this street more than happy to give me their brush.

HENRIETTA. Good, then go and get one, maybe they'll learn you what it's meant to be used for... and Thomas, be you in by ten.

THOMAS. Right.

THOMAS *leaves*.

HENRIETTA. You don't have youngins.

ELSPETH. Are you thinking, it's easy for me, I have no children, and I have the luxury of doing all this.

HENRIETTA. No... the opposite, I did what I did for my weeins... especially the two wee lassies, they are only six and eight, but I had hopes, God help me, that maybe this place will be better for them... if I had no weeins, don't know if I would bother. Go through all this for me...? I admire you... you do what you do for all of us... I don't know if I could be that person.

ELSPETH. You know the real reason I came here, because I believed I could change your mind... I thought, Henrietta is different, she won't be led by anybody, she won't give in.

HENRIETTA. You have to carry on for me... don't give up, still fight on, be a tumour. I can't be of much use to you any more... upstart that he is, I have to stand by my son and the rest of my youngsters, but I will be watchin' and listenin' and deep down here I will be screamin' and shoutin' like I did in that court... and if you need to run from the police... this will be a safe house... my children won't breathe a word... this is the one place where I have all the say, all the power, and by God I will use it.

ELSPETH. Thank you, Henrietta... I'll go.

HENRIETTA. Go this way, through the back door to the entry, it's dark but you just keep goin' straight and it will get to the main road by the tram stop... wait a minute.

HENRIETTA *goes to a chest and gets a large shawl.*

Put this over you and give me that bloody hat and I'll wrap it in newspaper... that's a dead giveaway.

ELSPETH. Keep it, there's plenty more where that came from.

HENRIETTA. Me, keep this, catch yerself on, when would I have occasion to wear this?

ELSPETH. You might need it for the next court case... please, keep it.

HENRIETTA *takes the hat and sets it on the table.*

The sound of marching getting close.

HENRIETTA. Go on, and remember, this house is here if you need it, I'll be here if you need me... if bloody Sir Edward Carson as a Member of Parliament can smuggle illegal arms, call for civil war and not get arrested, then I can break laws in his house, this is my parliament... that way, me and him is equal.

ELSPETH *hugs her, puts the shawl over her head and leaves.*

HENRIETTA *contines to brush the boots... the marching gets louder... the rhythm of the brushing eventually fuses with the timing of the march... fade lights on this.*

The End.

THE LIONESS

Rebecca Lenkiewicz

Rebecca Lenkiewicz is currently under commission to the National Theatre, London, and Manhattan Theatre Club, New York. *Her Naked Skin*, directed by Howard Davies, premiered at the National Theatre in 2008, the first play to be performed on the Olivier stage by a living female playwright. *The Night Season*, also at the National Theatre, won the Critics' Circle Most Promising Playwright Award, 2004. Other work includes *Soho – A Tale of Table Dancers* (Arcola Theatre/British Council tour); *Shoreditch Madonna* (Soho Theatre); *Blue Moon Over Poplar* (NYT/Soho Theatre); *The Soldier's Tale* (Old Vic Theatre); *An Enemy of the People* (Arcola Theatre); and *Faeries* (Royal Opera House). Rebecca's new version of Ibsen's *Ghosts* was produced by ATC at the Arcola Theatre in 2009. Rebecca also writes for radio and television.

Characters

ELIZABETH I, *from age twenty-five to sixty-eight*
JOHN KNOX, *forty-five, Scottish*
ESSEX, *twenty-eight to thirty-four, English*
NEUZER, *a male doctor, from age thirty to seventy-one*

And COURTIERS

Scene One

London, 1560. ELIZABETH, *twenty-five, sits with a huge skirt on, under which her legs are parted very wide. She is concentrated as she is in slight pain but we would not be aware of this as she covers it with her thoughts – although her breathing might hint at it.*

ELIZABETH. I am almost born. My mother screams. My father hunts. He stands stock-still amongst the corn. Waiting. For quail. And for word of a son. Tournaments have been planned. A sound of feathers beating out of a bush. A messenger approaches. I am upon my mother's stomach, umbilically attached, abundant colours. I am smooth. Viscous. Bloodied. And blank between the legs. A grey storm cloud envelopes the yellow fields. Pa listens, nods slowly. The parties are cancelled.

Now there is movement under her skirt, somebody. ELIZABETH closes her eyes for a few moments while the movement continues, now she winces with pain.

No more.

DOCTOR NEUZER, *thirty, climbs out hurriedly from under* ELIZABETH'*s skirts.*

You have delved sufficiently into Gloriana, sir.

NEUZER. Majesty. I hope I did not pain you?

ELIZABETH. It is no matter.

NEUZER. I tried to be gentle. It is inevitably sensitive being such... virgin territory.

ELIZABETH. It is England's velvet. I shall be paraded around presently like a prize heifer. Ripe for market. For some Spanish steer. What do you want for in life, doctor?

NEUZER. I?

ELIZABETH. Wealth? The discovery of a new cure? What do you suppose I desire most? For my twenty-sixth birthday. What should I wish for?

NEUZER. Majesty… peace with the Catholics? Or a respite to the unrest in Ireland?

ELIZABETH. Quite. Thank you, doctor.

NEUZER. I noticed, Majesty, that there was inflammation around the area of the kidneys. Have you had any pain?

ELIZABETH. Possibly. If a person were to have such pain, what should they do about it?

NEUZER. They must calm the nerves. You should take long progresses in the summer. Walk gently. Meditate a little but do nothing strenuous.

ELIZABETH. I have had no pain. Thank you.

NEUZER *bows and leaves.* ELIZABETH *puts her hands to her stomach, she has a jab of pain from the internal examination she has undergone and an ache in her kidneys.*

My mother conceives again when I am a few months old. But she flushes and screams out an almost-boy who is more blood than body long before her term. At age one I am displayed naked to the French Ambassadors. Negotiations begin for an alliance and by the time I am two I have acquired a French suitor. My mother miscarries a second time. Careless of her, no? I am not yet three when my father kills my mother. No crime of passion. He plans the event and pays good money for it. He is in bed with sweet, pliant Jane as my mother's body enters rigor mortis and stiffens. Jane's nipples are rosebud pink against ivory skin. My mother's are purple hard berries against the palest of blue breasts. The blood has pooled internally around her knees and ankles. As though she wore maroon stockings. He accused my mother of having five lovers at court. Five, mark you, not four nor three but five. One for each of his short, fat, fingers. And one of them her brother. My, how men fantasise.

Scene Two

London, 1560. ELIZABETH *stands before her Privy Council,*
angry.

ELIZABETH. I asked about Ireland. And you do not answer me.

Silence. ELIZABETH *stares at her ministers.*

England is strong in itself. I refuse to be pandered to some
foreign prince. I am your anointed Queen. Not a royal
whore. You would do well to remember that.

No. No. No. Do I tell you who to bed? Or demand you to
sire a child? I tell you I will never be constrained to do anything. And I am endowed with such qualities that if I were
turned out of this realm in my petticoat I were able to live in
any place in Christendom.

ELIZABETH *looks to the Council. She is unchallenged.*

Ireland, Dudley, who's wreaking what upon whom in Ulster?
And what word of Knox? Is he found?

Scene Three

London, 1560. ELIZABETH *sits in a window seat. Sunshine*
streams in. She closes her eyes and basks in it for a few
moments. KNOX *stands before her, his head bowed.*

ELIZABETH. When I was a child, my father often wore
yellow. You know why you are here?

ELIZABETH *opens her eyes now and looks at* KNOX.
ELIZABETH *motions slightly with her head and* KNOX
takes a few steps away from her.

KNOX. Majesty.

ELIZABETH. My little brother was nine when he came to power. 'No one else fit to rule,' they said. I was his senior by four years. Sir. I do not like you.

KNOX. Majesty. I am not surprised.

ELIZABETH. What does surprise you, Mr Knox?

KNOX. How far from right man's spirit can travel.

ELIZABETH. And woman's?

KNOX. The female race are one suspended surprise to me.

ELIZABETH. Sit.

>KNOX *sits on a chair and* ELIZABETH *looks at him. He returns her gaze.*

>What do you see?

KNOX. Majesty.

ELIZABETH. You said that before. I read your book.

>*There is a moment of knowledge between them,* KNOX *senses deep trouble.*

KNOX. Majesty… I am flattered.

ELIZABETH. Unfortunately, I was not.

KNOX. Majesty…

ELIZABETH. That's all you seem able to say today, Mr Knox. Has the cat got your tongue?

KNOX. The tract is against the danger of Catholics.

ELIZABETH. Remind me of its title?

>KNOX *looks at her, he knows that she must remember the title.*

>I wish to hear it from the author's lips.

KNOX. 'The First Blast of the Trumpet Against the Monstrous Regiment of Women.'

ELIZABETH *picks up a copy to hand and looks at it.*

ELIZABETH. There are more to come then? More blasts? Or at least a sequel? Are you proud of it?

KNOX. Pride is for a parent not an author.

ELIZABETH. I am a parent myself. Of England. I am mother to every little bastard in the country. Whether they be good or wretched. It is not easy being King.

KNOX. Majesty, the protest was truly against the Catholics and not women.

ELIZABETH. Then the title is a gross lie. We kill liars in England. When their sedition is harmful. Perhaps you do not notice them north of the border... Am I part of this 'monstrous regiment of women'?

KNOX. You have ruled like a true king in your reign so far.

ELIZABETH. Read where I have marked.

KNOX *takes the book, nods, looks at the passage, prepares himself...*

KNOX. 'How abominable before God is the Empire or Rule of a wicked woman, yea of a traitresse and bastard.'

ELIZABETH. Am I a traitresse?

KNOX. It refers to Mary Tudor.

ELIZABETH. You throw stones at a dead woman.

KNOX. She was very much alive when I wrote it. And killed a great many Protestants.

ELIZABETH. Your friend was amongst those whom were martyred.

KNOX. Wishart was an exemplary man.

ELIZABETH. And you watched him burn?

KNOX. Yes. I did.

ELIZABETH *nods. She no longer wishes to speak, she is not weary but 'stopped'.*

We are in...

ELIZABETH *stops his speech with her hand.* KNOX *stops.* ELIZABETH *pauses and now comes back to him.*

ELIZABETH. Yes?

KNOX. We are in constant danger of Catholic subversion from within, or encirclement from without. I simply endeavour to fly the Protestant flag.

ELIZABETH. Read.

KNOX. 'To promote a woman to bear rule is... repugnant to nature... it is the subversion of good order, of all equity and justice. It is against God.'

ELIZABETH. And yet God has made me King. Why would he do so if I sin against him?

KNOX. It was the papists I was aiming at.

ELIZABETH. For a writer, you are inept with words. Proceed.

KNOX. 'Their sight in civil regiment is but blindness; their strength, weakness; their counsel foolishness and judgement frenzy if it rightly be considered.'

ELIZABETH. You quote St Paul, citing that females are both 'the port and gate of the devil'. And then St Augustine who says that 'woman ought to be repressed and bridled betimes, if she aspire to any dominion'.

KNOX. I was not railing against your brilliant self.

ELIZABETH. You'd like to see us swum as witches, wouldn't you?

KNOX. No.

ELIZABETH. Or burnt perhaps?

KNOX. Truly, no.

ELIZABETH. I was shown the Skeffington's Gyves yesterday. Have you seen it?

KNOX. I have, Your Majesty. It breaks the back, does it not?

ELIZABETH. It compresses the body so that it resembles nothing less than a broken ball.

KNOX. I should like to know if I am on trial here?

ELIZABETH. One expends time and energy on a trial. You are worthy of neither. You wish my tribe to crack or to become hunchback, Knox. Or best of all to disappear. But I shall be a good queen. And king.

KNOX. What will become of my publication, Majesty?

ELIZABETH. Your work is less than a woman's rag. It is simply human waste. A fiction. The only remarkable fact is that someone agreed to print it.

KNOX. It was of Mary that I wrote.

ELIZABETH. You cannot say my sister's name without blanching. You believe that Mary Tudor was a tyrant?

KNOX. What that woman was, I forbear for respect to say.

ELIZABETH. Leave your respect outside. Speak freely.

KNOX. She was a daughter of sedition. A bloodthirsty virago.

ELIZABETH. She had many followers.

KNOX. The people will generally support who is in power.

ELIZABETH. When Mary was dying, her acolytes jammed the roads to Hatfield to present themselves to me. She was buried alive long before she died. Were you here for my accession?

KNOX. No.

ELIZABETH. They lit a thousand bonfires. I sailed down the Thames in a golden barge. You would think that decadent?

KNOX. You were Cleopatra for a night.

ELIZABETH. I was Elizabeth. They cut the red carpet I walked down into hundreds of pieces and sent them around the country. Wonderfully sumptuous idolatry. Does Wishart haunt you?

KNOX. Yes.

ELIZABETH. My mother was put to death when I was three. She visits me occasionally. We are then perhaps both haunted. How does one rid one's self of the ghost?

KNOX. Prayer.

ELIZABETH. I have tried it. Doesn't work.

ELIZABETH *motions for the book back.* KNOX *gives it to her.*

Why do you hate women?

KNOX. I don't.

ELIZABETH. Fear them then?

KNOX. No.

ELIZABETH. It's curious that we are the one species who has coitus not just to procreate, no?

KNOX, *awkward, cannot find an answer.*

Women continue to mate when they are become barren. And they retain their bosom whose true function is done with. I watched a stag and deer once. Rutting. She looked terribly unenthusiastic. It was all about the rump. But we are designed to be face to face for the most part, wouldn't you say? How is your Church of Scotland faring?

KNOX. It is blooming. Thank you, Majesty.

ELIZABETH. Never thank me for anything, Knox. I never gave you aught and I never shall. Is that clear? You have found no remedy to rid you of the dead?

KNOX. Truly I have not.

ELIZABETH. Then you are of less use to me than your lunatic pap is to true literature. Begone.

KNOX. Yes, Majesty.

ELIZABETH. If you write such invertebrate bile again I shall play Herod. And have your head upon a plate. And your prick sawn from you and spiked upon a bayonet.

KNOX. Yes, Your Majesty. You are too kind.

ELIZABETH. I am.

> KNOX *leaves.* ELIZABETH *sits and puts her hands to her neck. Around her neck, rubs her neck then stops.* ELIZABETH *breathes hard, almost a light panic attack.*

Scene Four

London, 1587. ELIZABETH, *fifty-two, circles* ESSEX, *twenty-two, who sits waiting for her.* ELIZABETH *talks to us as she looks at* ESSEX, *who is not 'there' as yet.*

ELIZABETH. I am fifty-two. Time flies. I have forgotten completely my mother's face. But on my person I wear a ring which conceals a miniature of her opposite one of myself. Her daughter has steered England away from war and debt. I am Diana, Gloriana, the Faerie Queene. My face is whiter than Dover. As are my hands. Except... except that they are not. So very white. They are bloodied.

> ELIZABETH *runs her fingers through* ESSEX's *hair. She touches his cheek, blows the hair out of his face. She smiles, kisses him, but she is not really 'there'. Now she snaps back into reality and addresses* ESSEX.

You're too generous, Robert.

ESSEX. Don't berate me. I ask favours for my friends as anyone would.

ELIZABETH. They would not. They would think of themselves. Every day you plead their cases.

ESSEX. Because you can give so much, Bess, and it affects you so little... Why are you smiling? I thought this was a dressing down.

ELIZABETH. I am not in an angry vein. Have you seen the new portrait of me?

ESSEX. Yes. It's very fine.

ELIZABETH. Did you notice the rainbow I'm clutching? I hold it next to my thigh. I think it looks rather obscene.

ESSEX. I must give it a second look. You seem more yourself. Has it lifted a little?

ELIZABETH. Perhaps. I slept a few hours for the first time last night. It's... a strange time. You have no fear of me, do you?

ESSEX. No.

ELIZABETH. Good.

ELIZABETH *sits. She is very concentrated, looking out of a window.* ESSEX *takes a blanket and puts it around her.*

ESSEX. Bess? You're shivering. England must not get a chill.

ELIZABETH. They say her little dog hid under her skirts, Rob. It would not leave her after she was dead.

ESSEX. It's probably a story.

ELIZABETH. If they're making up myths about her then that's even worse.

ESSEX. They're not. It's done. And they say it had to be so.

ELIZABETH. Do you condemn me for it?

ESSEX. No.

ELIZABETH. I don't know what to do with the body. The room in which she's kept savours so strong that they are talking of it.

ESSEX. We must bury her and soon. We'll give her a fitting funeral or there'll be riots. James will raise all hell if his mother's not laid somewhere decent.

ELIZABETH. I can't go, Robert. I just can't.

ESSEX. No. You mustn't. Send a few important people along. Bedford, Lincoln, Rutland. Get rid of some bores for a few days. Buy dresses for a hundred poor women.

ELIZABETH. Do you think they sew the head back on to be put in the coffin?

ESSEX. God knows.

ELIZABETH. I often wondered that when I was a child. When I tried to imagine my mother. I would go to sleep wondering whether she was buried in two parts or one. I must hole up for a while. I must not be seen to worry or weaken.

ESSEX. Don't worry about the Council. Let them think what they like. Do exactly as you would, Bess.

ELIZABETH. I am not free. I do not live in a corner. A thousand eyes see all I do. Do the people love me?

ESSEX. They worship you.

ELIZABETH. They thought nothing of me before I came to the throne.

ESSEX. You've ruled for three decades.

ELIZABETH. Do not tell anyone that I am prone to melancholy, will you?

ESSEX. I would rather die upon my own sword.

ELIZABETH. No need for drama, Rob. Just… discretion. Do you talk about me with your wife?

ESSEX. No.

ELIZABETH. Never leave me, will you? Even if I try to push you away. I should die if you were to fear me.

ELIZABETH *has a severe pain in the head and in her kidney.*

ESSEX. Elizabeth, what is it? You're ill?

ELIZABETH. It will pass. Would you hold me? For a moment?

ESSEX *holds* ELIZABETH *very gently. She breathes. He smoothes her back carefully and they breathe together.*

Everybody leaves, Robert. There is no constant. It's like the stars. The constellations. Bodies turning endlessly. No one stands still.

ESSEX. You are the heat of the sun, Bess. We are all chaos and the spheres. Jangling and worrying around you. I'm sorry. That I cannot take your sadness away.

ELIZABETH. I have seen so much. Tell no one but I am tired.

ESSEX. Has the pain gone?

ELIZABETH. The bite of it. An ache remains.

ESSEX. Sit upon my knee a while. Let me take the royal weight off your sovereign feet.

ESSEX *sits upon a chair and* ELIZABETH *sits upon his knee.*

ELIZABETH. Am I too heavy for you?

ESSEX. Light as a feather.

ELIZABETH. Were you a happy child, Rob?

ESSEX. I doubt it. You?

ELIZABETH. I doubt it. Funny creatures, aren't we? I do not mind for myself now. But as a girl.

ESSEX. What would you have had that you did not?

ELIZABETH. I would have liked to have gone a-maying. Plain dress. Plain face. A country fayre.

ESSEX. Cider. A fire. Fiddles playing. No trumpets. No castrati. Just a few rustic voices.

They laugh. ESSEX *sings a snatch of a country song as he gently rocks* ELIZABETH.

ELIZABETH. And so we are. Through my months of insomnia. He stays each night till the birds start to sing. And more and more he moves me. And my autumn is made magnificent through his summer. But blossom is delicate. It bruises... How quickly the world doth shift. And yet so gradual that we persuade ourselves it is a natural occurrence... and besides I must endure the childish dealings of war.

Scene Five

Tilbury, 1588. ELIZABETH *addresses the troops.*

ELIZABETH. My loving people, let tyrants fear. I have come among you not for my recreation and disport, but being resolved, in the midst and the heat of the battle, to live or die amongst you all. To lay down for my God, and for my Kingdom, and for my people, my honour and my blood, even in the dust. I know I have the body but of a weak and feeble woman, but I have the heart and stomach of a king and of a King of England too, and think foul scorn that Parma or Spain, or any Prince of Europe should dare to invade the borders of my realm. If this should happen I myself will take up arms, I myself will be your general, judge and rewarder... and I... I am not afraid of anything.

Scene Six

London, 1594. ELIZABETH *and* ESSEX *stare at each other.*
Two COURTIER*S are also present.*

ESSEX. You can't refuse me more troops!

ELIZABETH. I can and I do, sir. You have made a mockery of
those I sent you. Ireland is as great a mess now as when you
arrived there. Possibly worse. You march and you march and
you camp and decamp but no progress is made!

ESSEX. I need more soldiers! And people I can trust must serve
beside me!

ELIZABETH. Do not shout, sir. I hear your words quite clearly.

ESSEX. Elizabeth…

ELIZABETH. Majesty…

ESSEX. This is a farce!

ELIZABETH. If there is a farcical element it is you who supply
it. You gave out twenty-one knighthoods in a week, sir? You
hand them out as though they were figs. You use your sword
more often to dub than to fight.

ESSEX. Do not give me the power to bestow unless you wish
me to use it.

ELIZABETH. Restraint is something you never learnt, my Earl
of Essex.

ESSEX. And I thank God for it! Look at them! Terrified to
speak their minds and wanting to show the Queen every
minutiae of their achievements. If you thought your piss
would please the Queen you would bottle it and wrap it in a
red ribbon.

ELIZABETH. Robert!

ESSEX (*to the* COURTIERS). Give us the place alone!

ELIZABETH. Stay! You do not rule here, sir!

ESSEX. Puppets! Your Majesty knows me. Intimately. I am not an indigent. Neither am I grasping. Money leaves me cold. I only ask for more support and a few titles for my loved ones.

ELIZABETH. You spend enough for one who is not partial to money.

ESSEX. Do not belittle yourself, Elizabeth. That was low.

ELIZABETH. I? Belittle? I hold the lives of the English people on a knife edge. Daily. You have no idea of real work. Or procedure. You call meetings with your cohorts at all hours and in all places.

ESSEX. You record me? I had rather live in the country free than be spied upon, Bess.

ELIZABETH. I am told by my source that one conference took place in your bed.

ESSEX. And you are angry that you were not invited?

ELIZABETH *hits* ESSEX. *His natural instinct is to draw his sword. The* COURTIERS *are upon him and hold him.*

FIRST COURTIER. Majesty!

SECOND COURTIER. We have him, My Queen.

ESSEX. She is not yours. You are not hers. God's death, we are people, are we not? Individuals! Tell them to unhand me.

ELIZABETH *nods.* ESSEX *lays his sword at her feet.*

I am deeply sorry, Majesty. Forgive. I had not expected a blow and there is a dog-like reaction in me. If I am struck my hand goes to my sword as others' hands might go to their face. Forgive. There was no thought. My blood was up. I would rather be flayed alive than inflict a single scratch upon your fair skin. I love you.

ELIZABETH *nods.*

I am not afeared of poverty. I have taken such a taste of the rural that I could happily retire there.

ELIZABETH. We know, my Earl of Essex. You were impoverished. You repeat the story oft.

ESSEX. I will retire to some cell in the country, Bess. I shall live there and I shall never be desirous to look a good man in the face again.

ELIZABETH. Yes. You say that every time. And yet you still come back.

ELIZABETH *motions for them all to go*.

England shall be alone.

They make to leave. ESSEX *bows low and tries to kiss* ELIZABETH*'s hand but she takes it from him*.

Do you hear me? Alone!

They leave.

Again…

Scene Seven

London, 1601. ELIZABETH *addresses the people*.

ELIZABETH. To be a king and wear a crown is a thing more glorious to them that see it than it is pleasant to them that bear it. It is not my desire to live nor reign longer than my life and reign shall be your good. And though you have had, and may have, many mightier and wiser princes sitting in this seat, yet you never had, nor shall have, any that will love you better.

ELIZABETH *waves to the crowds. She walks away from the public and into her private corner*.

He came to me once. Rushed into my room in the morning. 'Bess!' he shouted, 'I must see you!' As though he were my lover. I was half-dressed and my wig was not on. He saw me then. My true age. My scalp and grizzled hair. He tried not to stare. So little imagination he had. He thought I awoke as a Rainbow Goddess. Treason followed. As naturally as night follows day. And yet so unnatural that I puked every night at the thought of his imprisonment.

Scene Eight

London, 1601. ELIZABETH *visits* ESSEX *in the Tower. They are silent a while.*

ELIZABETH. You have no words.

ESSEX. My crime is a leprosy, Majesty.

ELIZABETH. You rode through the streets armed.

ESSEX. We were carried away. Angry. But we were not contemplating violence. I would never lay a finger upon you except to protect you. Bess? You know that, don't you? Or I shall go insane.

ELIZABETH. Lee pleaded your case. He wouldn't stop. We hanged him.

ESSEX. I have a request.

ELIZABETH. You always have one. And then another. I have indulged you as though you were my child.

ESSEX. Or your lover.

ELIZABETH. Go careful, Robert.

ESSEX. What have I to lose? I am going to the block.

ELIZABETH. You are a mad ingrate. You have at last made apparent what for so long has been hidden in your mind. And yes, you must prepare yourself for your God.

ESSEX. Southampton should be spared.

ELIZABETH. You are no longer my adviser. You are a prisoner.

ESSEX. That makes me no less of a man. You were a prisoner here too.

ELIZABETH. But I had not betrayed one who gave me all. They said you've been ill.

ESSEX. It was nothing. It was the damp.

ELIZABETH. It is cold.

ESSEX. I need you to forgive me.

ELIZABETH. I found it hard to sleep when I was here. The nights were full of noises. If it wasn't the screams it was the animals. The monkeys. The bears. I arrived here by boat. They took my hand and they led me through the gate.

ESSEX. How old were you?

ELIZABETH. Twenty.

ESSEX. A child. I should have liked to know you then. Were you frightened?

ELIZABETH. No. I was angry. It was pouring with rain and I stopped them from leading me inside the walls. I sat myself down upon the wet earth. I shouted. I said, 'It is better sitting here than in a worse place!' And then my old usher, he started to cry. And I suddenly thought that the crowds might interpret my sit-down protest as fear. So I stood up and looked at them all. And just as I did, a great lion's roar came from the keep. And I smiled and walked in.

ESSEX. It was a lioness. She recognised your strength.

ELIZABETH. You laughed during the indictment.

ESSEX. When they talked of my wanting to destroy you. It was too ridiculous.

ELIZABETH. They gave me the death warrant.

ESSEX *nods*.

It is signed.

ESSEX. By whom?

ELIZABETH. I have signed it.

ESSEX. That is sudden.

ELIZABETH. Your request. I cannot grant it.

ESSEX. My request?

ELIZABETH. It is impossible to forgive you.

ESSEX. It wasn't that. I would like it to happen privately. The execution. Please.

ELIZABETH. I… cannot.

ESSEX. Please.

ELIZABETH. It's not within my… power.

ESSEX *takes this in*.

ESSEX. Very well. Will I be allowed to speak?

ELIZABETH. Of course.

ESSEX. A psalm then.
    'With your great mercy wipe away my crimes.
    Thoroughly wash my transgressions away,
    And cleanse me from my offence.
    For my crimes I know,
    And my offence is before me always.'

ELIZABETH. 'Purify me with a hyssop, that I be clean.
    Wash me, that I be whiter than snow.
    Let me hear gladness and joy,
    Let the bones that you crush exult.'

ESSEX *nods.*

ESSEX. 'A broken spirit. A broken, crushed heart God spurns not.'

ESSEX *takes* ELIZABETH*'s hand.* ELIZABETH *takes it away from him and leaves.*

Scene Nine

London, 1601. ELIZABETH *sits, waiting.* NEUZER *lets her blood.*

ELIZABETH. What do you do, sir?

NEUZER. I am letting a tiny amount of your blood, Majesty.

ELIZABETH. Will you sell it?

NEUZER. No.

ELIZABETH. Then you're a fool. It would fetch a good price.

NEUZER. They tell me you will not sleep.

ELIZABETH. If I lie down I shall not rise again.

NEUZER. Lift your arm a little for me, please, Majesty.

ELIZABETH. Have you heard a shot?

NEUZER. For the Earl of Essex? There has been none, Majesty.

ELIZABETH. You are sure?

NEUZER. Quite. There was a large crowd.

ELIZABETH. The masses will always come out for a murder.

NEUZER. Cough if it please you, Your Majesty.

ELIZABETH. It does not. If you want me to cough then tell me to.

NEUZER. Cough.

ELIZABETH *coughs. And it hurts her to do so. She tries to regain her composure.*

ELIZABETH. They say that when my cousin was killed her mouth kept moving for a full quarter-hour after the axe went down. Is that possible? Medically?

NEUZER. Certainly the body can enter spasms after the heart has stopped. Just as a chicken will run after it is beheaded.

ELIZABETH. Her orisons in Latin were so loud in her last moments that they drowned out the Dean. Was that faith or fear, do you think?

A shot fires. ELIZABETH *feels it to the very core of her body.*

NEUZER. Majesty?

ELIZABETH *nods, she cannot speak.*

Your Highness? Can I get you something?

ELIZABETH *shakes her head. She needs to cry.*

ELIZABETH. Show me your hands.

NEUZER *shows her his hands. She looks at them gently.*

No trace. No trace of me. Leave me.

NEUZER. Majesty.

NEUZER *bows and leaves.*

ELIZABETH. You called me Bess... I wish we could go a-maying, Robert. That I was a girl in a field. With your body atop of mine. And when I look up there is just you. And the sky. Poppies surround us. A little blood trickles from between my legs. A gentle pain that is so sweet. Take me a-maying, Rob. I shall stop having bad dreams and we will conquer a world. A small and beautiful empire. A barn. Make love to me. Please. Please Robert. 'A broken spirit. A broken, crushed heart God spurns not.' Love me. Rob...? Love me.

Blackout.

HANDBAGGED

Moira Buffini

Moira Buffini is currently Writer-in-Residence at the National Theatre Studio. Her writing for theatre includes *Dinner* (2002) for the National Theatre; *Loveplay* (2001) for the RSC, which was nominated for an Olivier Award for Best Comedy; *Silence* (1999), Birmingham Rep and Plymouth Theatre Royal, winner of the Susan Smith Blackburn Prize; *Gabriel* (1997), for Soho Theatre, winner of LWT Award and Whiting Award; and *Blatvasky's Tower* (Fringe).

More recently, Moira wrote *Dying for It*, a free adaptation of *The Suicide* by Nikolai Erdman, and *Marianne Dreams* based on Catherine Storr's book, both for the Almeida (2007). She also wrote *A Vampire Story*, for the National Theatre's Connections Festival (2008). Her latest play, *Welcome to Thebes,* opened on the National Theatre Olivier stage in June 2010. Moira has also written a screen adaptation of *A Vampire Story* for Number 9 Films, an adaptation of *Jane Eyre* for BBC and Ruby Films for theatrical release, and a screen adaptation of *Tamara Drewe* for Ruby Films, directed by Stephen Frears.

Characters

MRS THATCHER (T)
QUEEN ELIZABETH II (Q)
MAGS
LIZ
RONALD REAGAN (RON)
SHEA

MRS THATCHER (T). *She is very elderly. She prepares to address us.*

T   Freedom and democracy
They are things worth dying for
And we must never
Never stop resisting those
Who would take them from us.
The act of resistance is our defining act as human
      beings.
To say 'No, I will not stand for that,'
To say 'No, I will not do this thing you ask of me
      because I know it's wrong.' To say 'No, I
      won't collude, collaborate, negotiate. I will
      have no part of it.'
To shout out to the enemies of freedom
'You are wrong.'
To resist, whatever the cost
Even if it be your life.

To say 'No'

This is courage
This is true integrity.
I would be proud if this word defined me:

'NO'

I'd like a chair
I don't need one but I'd like one
I will not ask for one
If I wait, they will notice
They will bring me one
One of the little people
One of the men
Dancing around me in their suits

Neat cuffs, ties flapping in the wind.
Holding their documents like babies

The men
I could pin them wriggling with my gaze
And then release them with a smile.
Secretly, I liked to do it.
Girlish.
I was girlish.

QUEEN ELIZABETH II (Q) *enters dragging a chair. She is elderly.*

Q   You look as if you need a chair

T   I'm quite capable of standing, thank you, ma'am

Q   I'm bringing you a chair

T   There really isn't any need

She places it.

Q   Here

T   No, thank you

Q   I've gone and brought it now, sit down

T   I'd rather stand

They both stand.

Q   We conceive parliamentary institutions, with their free speech and respect for the rights of minorities, to be a precious part of our way of life and outlook. They inspire a broad tolerance in thought and expression

During recent centuries, this message has been sustained and invigorated by the immense contribution, in language, literature, and action, of the nations of our Commonwealth. The Commonwealth gives expression, as I pray it always will, to living principles. I ask

you now to cherish them – and practise them too; then we can go forward together in peace, seeking justice and freedom for all men.
God bless you all

T   Why don't you sit down?

Q   No, thank you

They both stand.

What can one say here? How far can one go?

T   Oh, don't hold back
           It's all beyond our control

Q   Indeed
           All artifice and sham
           I've never liked the theatre

T   No

Q   We saw *War Horse* recently
           We liked the horses
           Would you like tea?

T   Tea
           Would be very nice

A younger Queen (LIZ) *and a younger Thatcher* (MAGS) *enter.*

MAGS   We knew we had won by the early hours of May the 4th. I can remember an odd sense of loneliness when I received the call which summoned me to the Palace. The audience, at which one receives the Queen's authority to form a government, comes only once in a lifetime.

LIZ   Anyone who imagines that this authority's a mere formality or lightly given is quite wrong. It is a unique and vital part of Britain's democratic heritage

T	I never said there is no such thing as society

Q   Yes, you did. It was in *Woman's Own*

T   Society is a framework for freedom
        Freedom that gives a man room to breathe…
        To make his own decisions and to chart his own
            course.
        There is the individual
        And there is family
        There is no such thing

Q   As responsible government
        That's how you sounded
        No such thing as an obligation to the people
        No such thing as Britain

T   There's no such thing as entitlement
        People in this country feel entitled
        If they have a problem, it's the Government that
            has to put it right
        'I'm homeless, the Government must house me – '
            why?
        The Government is not responsible for all
            society's ills

Q   Does one then condemn the homeless?

T   That is a matter for the homeless to decide

MAGS   I found the Monarch's attitude

LIZ   I found the Prime Minister's attitude

MAGS   Towards the working of Government

LIZ   Towards the working of Monarchy

MAGS ⎫ Absolutely correct
LIZ ⎭ Absolutely correct

LIZ   Every week, for all the years she was in office, the
            Prime Minister and I would meet

MAGS   Usually on a Tuesday

A brief audience

LIZ We would discuss two or three subjects of interest
to us both

MAGS And we would drink a cup of tea

LIZ Our meetings were private

MAGS We never took notes
And Her Majesty would have no one else in the
room

LIZ We are the only two who know what was said

T Of course, stories about clashes

Q There was never any question

T Stories about clashes

Q Nonsense

T There was never any question

Q We have got on very well with all of our Prime
Ministers

MAGS Into the Palace I would go
A man or two somewhere behind
Shadowy faces
Briefing me in the car
– Not that I needed it –
Up the staircase
To an underheated and exquisite room

T I liked the fact that it was cold
I respected that
We could have been –

LIZ The first time she came to the Palace
Leader of the Opposition then
She got overexcited and fainted clean away

T I didn't faint
I was not excited

LIZ	The second time she complained of dizziness. 'Is she going to keel over again?' I asked the man at my side
MAGS	I was unwell I retreated to the lavatory
LIZ	We didn't take it personally. My husband made a quip about tight control underwear
Q	No he did not
LIZ	With my previous Prime Ministers There was a gallantry A mutual letting down of hair They were all older than me And each in his own way Quite charming Even Edward Heath
Q	My first was Winston He met me on the tarmac when my father died He said some very lovely things
T	'Famous have been the reigns of our queens' I heard it on the wireless that night. 'Some of the greatest periods in history Have unfolded under their sceptre' Dennis and I were very moved. 'A new Elizabethan age… '
LIZ	And here was Mrs Thatcher
MAGS	She's impeccable
LIZ	She's jolly well groomed
MAGS } LIZ	She's six months younger She's six months older
Q	She had fought and won A woman My husband thought it quite astonishing And I suppose we had some things in common

	We were of the same era Formed in the war We both laboured for our nation
T	In every way we were peers

MAGS *curtsies*.

LIZ	Britain's first elected female leader
T	Of course, I don't notice that I'm a woman I regard myself as / Prime Minister
LIZ	(*Greeting her.*) Prime Minister
MAGS	Your Majesty
Q	Her curtsey was astonishingly deep
LIZ	Let's sit down

They sit.

	I liked your prayer last week On the steps of Number 10
MAGS	Oh yes, St Francis
T	I said where there is discord, may we bring harmony Where there is error, may we bring truth Where there is doubt, may we bring faith
LIZ	What exactly did you mean by it? Did you mean the Conservatives will bring those things Because truth and faith are tricky things to evoke
Q	I didn't say that. I said
LIZ	Journalists and policemen are always so big One finds them enormous They rather crowded you, I thought
MAGS	Yes, they rather did
LIZ	Yet you kept your self-possession Admirably

MAGS   Thank you
        I am used to the hustle and the bustle

LIZ   It'll only get hustlier
        And bustlier I'm sure

MAGS   I've lived the life of politics
        Since I was twenty-five

LIZ   You were a scientist before that?

MAGS   First scientist to be PM

LIZ   How admirable
        One was very keen on engineering in the war

MAGS   I was a research chemist
        I worked briefly for Lyons
        Developing methods to preserve ice cream
        And make it fluffier

LIZ   How yummy

MAGS   But I was also studying law
        And mothering twins
        Cooking Dennis breakfast
        You know how it is?

        LIZ *politely sips.*

        Then of course the politics took over
        I think I breathe it now

LIZ   Your voice changed, you know
        On the television
        When they asked about your father
        It became much softer

MAGS   Well, I owe him everything
        I really do

LIZ   One's relationship with one's father shapes one
            rather, doesn't it?

MAGS   It's passionately interesting to me
        That the things I learnt in a small town

                    In a very modest home
                    Are just the things
                    Which won us the election

LIZ   You must tell us how you like your tea
                    And whether biscuits are enough for you
                    We like Jacob's Chocolate Fingers

MAGS   Ma'am
                    I'm happy with a cup of tea

LIZ   You're lucky in a way
                    As PM you are not required to smile
                    I am, you see
                    And if one tries to smile for two hours
                            continuously
                    It gives one a nervous tic
                    One's face looks rather grumpy in repose
                    And the moment one stops smiling, someone says
                    'Doesn't she look cross?'

MAGS   I've been called far worse than cross

Q   Milk snatcher

MAGS   But one learns not to listen
                    Not to be affected

LIZ   Prime Minister
                    One likes to know what's going on

MAGS   Indeed

LIZ   One must remain impartial

MAGS   Absolutely

LIZ   So one likes to feel that one's a sort of sponge
                    You can come and tell me things
                    And some things stay
                    And some go out the other ear
                    But one just knows.
                    And occasionally
                    One can put one's point of view

MAGS	That is such an honour, ma'am
LIZ	One is unelected, yes But one likes to be constructive
MAGS	Oh, Your Majesty

LIZ	And of course, one is the Head of the
	    Commonwealth
	One has a great affection for all the member states
	And perhaps because one cannot publicly express
	    opinion
	One can be a useful tool
	Especially abroad
	One's perhaps like an emollient, I think
	One sometimes smoothes the way

MAGS	Yes This is a lovely service
Q	Was she listening?
LIZ	It was my great-great-grandma's
T	Queen Victoria's
MAGS	How very nice
T	You have no idea what it meant for me Meeting you on such an equal footing Taking tea Discussing state affairs I imagined my father What he would feel His pride in me…
LIZ	Will you be bringing any pets to Number 10?
	MAGS *is silent*.
Q	I thought if she's got a dog we've got a subject
LIZ	There was no intimacy with her
MAGS	I think she found my tongue-tied loyalty quite

Q	No letting down of hair
MAGS	Pets?
T	You are my Queen I am your subject The first move towards a close relationship Could not have come from me
MAGS	And you never made it
T	On my way back to Number 10 A thought stayed there insistently Despite my every effort to dispel it
MAGS	She'd made me feel the grocer's daughter
Q	We did not You're absolutely incorrect
T	I had worked so hard for my achievements Her Majesty's were birthrights
Q	I have to accept that here I am And this is my fate
MAGS	Fate has nothing to do with me It is all discipline and enterprise
LIZ	I thought her quite a snob If truth be known

Tea is over.

RONALD REAGAN *enters*.

RON	If I were there, Margaret, I'd throw my hat in the door before I came in
T	Ron There's no need to do that
Q	Of course, President Reagan and I had something big in common
Q, LIZ, R	Horses

Q	I don't watch many films. But when I met him I had to confess that I'd enjoyed every minute of *The Cattle Queen of Montana*
T	I preferred him in *Dark Victory* A small role but you could see such potential He dazzled Humphrey Bogart off the screen
MAGS	If he hadn't enlisted he would have been a huge, huge star
Q	He rode like an American, I thought That ease they have Not quite upright in the saddle but a certain grace
LIZ	Quite wonderful the chats we had We showed him all around our stud
T	We had a shared love too We shared a vision of the world A world free from the scourge of Communism What a communion of great ideals it was
Q	After his visit I sent him three eighteenth-century Worcester dishes
MAGS	I sent him a musical box It plays 'A Pair of Sparkling Eyes'
RON	Margaret, thank you very much for coming out of your debate to speak with me. I regret very much the embarrassment caused you.
LIZ	He invaded Grenada
Q	I am Head of State in Grenada
LIZ	Nobody told me As Head of State That Grenada was being invaded
T	I didn't know either, ma'am
MAGS	And I wasn't very happy I can tell you

RON	We met in pyjamas out in the living room of our suite because of this urgent appeal for support from Grenada and the eastern Caribbean states
LIZ	That's not how it happened Our people told us
Q	He invaded first And then extracted the appeal for support
MAGS	Well, Ron, I was upset.
RON	Your last communication was a little hot
MAGS	I have no wish to damage our friendship
RON	Hell no
MAGS	Told me the whole story in such conciliating terms
RON	When word came of your concerns – by the time I got it – the zero hour had passed, and our forces were already on their way. I feared a leak – not at your end but ours
MAGS	A leak?
RON	The time difference made it later in the day when you learned of it
Q	Time difference?
LIZ	Poppycock
T	The President can be managed Over time, I can manage him
RON	This security leak I can't say much but Cuba was involved We had to act with utmost speed
LIZ	This sets a wholly dangerous precedent Where else will he invade?
RON	We think that the military part is going to end very shortly

MAGS	That is very, very good news And then if we return to democracy that will be marvellous

RON	As I say, I'm sorry for any embarrassment that we
	     caused you, but please understand how much
	     we feared that leak

LIZ	No one spoke to us We had to ask for news We were so angry that we shouted at the dog
Q	Of course we didn't An absurd suggestion
MAGS	It's very kind of you to have rung, Ron
RON	Well, my pleasure
Q	Why didn't he ring me?
MAGS	How is Nancy?
RON	Just fine
MAGS	Do give her my love
RON	I shall
MAGS	And now I must return to this debate in the House. It's a bit tricky
RON	Alright, Margaret. Go get 'em. Eat 'em alive
MAGS	I will
T	I could see just the kind of man he was And I knew exactly what he needed

RON *comes forward.*

RON	I've got tremendous respect for both of those ladies My dealings with Britain are delightful And so easy I mean, they're any president's fantasy And I sure as hell never said that

MAGS   One forgets that she's Head of State in these little
        places
        In many ways it's a meaningless term

T   I managed Ron so successfully thereafter that he
        never even noticed it. A word in his ear, a
        memo of support, a trust. To anyone who says
        that my diplomacy was poor I give them this:
        we ended Communism. We brought down
        that wall

MAGS   And the Commonwealth – what is it really?
        A loose collection of underwhelming states.
        To put them on an equal footing with Great Britain
        is frankly –

RON   It's said that Queen Elizabeth was so angry at
        being ignored
        That when Margaret came for her audience that
        week
        She was not invited to sit down

LIZ   That's nonsense of course
        We've had a good relationship with all of our
        Prime Ministers
        We have a good relationship with everyone

RON   I admired the Queen more than I can say
        But to me there was only one Britannia

T   Oh Ron.

Q   It felt as if the Palace and I had been shifted –
        Bottom priority in your Number 10

LIZ   May one ask about the economy? Because it
        strikes one that the caps and the controls you
        have removed on our financial institutions

MAGS   The greater freedoms we have given

LIZ   Are widening the gap

MAGS   What gap?

Q   You're wilfully exacerbating social divisions at
            home and abroad

LIZ   I didn't say that, I said I've travelled a great deal
            this year as we do every year and we've seen,
            first hand, the growing gap.

MAGS   The wealth created will trickle down.

T   That Christmas I had indigestion
            To the consternation of my husband
            I was shouting at our television set

MAGS   No I wasn't

            The Queen's Speech:

LIZ   The greatest problem in the world today remains
            the gap between rich and poor countries

MAGS   What?

Q   My Christmas speech
            Jolly good one that year

LIZ   We can ignore the messages we don't like to hear
            but

MAGS   What's she talking about?

LIZ   We shall not begin to close this poverty gap until
            we hear less about nationalism and more
            about interdependence

MAGS   That is quite wrong

LIZ   One of the main aims of the Commonwealth is to
            make an effective contribution towards
            redressing the economic balance between
            nations

T   Dennis

MAGS   Dennis, she's flouting our policies
            The entire British effort is to distance ourselves –

LIZ   We in the Commonwealth are fortunate enough
To belong to a worldwide comradeship

MAGS }   *Comradeship?*
T   *Comradeship?*

LIZ   Let us make the most of it
Only then can we make the message of the angels
     come true:
'Peace on earth, goodwill towards men.'

MAGS   Good God

LIZ   I always look forward to being able to talk to
     everyone at Christmas time and at the end of
     another year I again send you all my warmest
     greetings

Q   God bless you all

T   Is Her Majesty
Queen of Great Britain and Northern Ireland
A Socialist?

Q   I hardly think so

MAGS   Then why, in her Christmas speech, is she
     expressing dubiously Socialistic principles?

Q   They are broadly speaking Christian principles
And as Head of the Church
One must freely express them

MAGS   Ma'am, you have done a great deal of travelling
     this year

LIZ   Yes and I have seen at first hand the enormous
     problems that poor countries face

T   She was sentimental

Q   Of course I wasn't
None of this was said
This is all crass surmise

MAGS	You have chosen to ally yourself with the Commonwealth
LIZ	One doesn't see a choice involved, Prime Minister One sees / one's duty
MAGS	If I may continue
LIZ	I believe I have a duty / as Head of the Commonwealth
MAGS	If I may, you have allied yourself Not with the British people But with a collection of nations Whom some regard as sycophants and mendicants
T	I never said that
Q	She cut me off She actually cut me off
T	Her Majesty had failed to realise that the nation's mood had changed
LIZ	There were no biscuits offered that night I can tell you
MAGS	The people do not care so very much about the Commonwealth
LIZ	How can you say so?
T	I didn't
Q	But you thought it You held the Commonwealth in contempt And that attitude trickled down The new free-market wealth did not
T	Something had changed in the decade We were unleashing new forces in the land Old orders everywhere were being questioned The unions, the NHS, the BBC and yes
Q	We were not protected from the media

The whole tone changed
No longer were the press respectful

T   The Palace did come under scrutiny

LIZ   Everything had to be value for money

Q   She sold our yacht, *Britannia*

LIZ   Thatcherism was a zealous creed

MAGS   I regard all those who want to destroy our way of
           life as Left

Q   Mrs Thatcher never, ever listened to another point
           of view

T   Of course I listened

Q   Her mind was always rigidly made up
           She was constantly crusading
           It could get very tiresome

LIZ   Attila the Hen
           I think that was Dennis Healy

Q   Who called her the Maggietollah?

T   Sometimes we got the feeling that the Palace
           found us funny
           Found our fervour for improvement somehow
           funny
           Hurtful

           MAGS *and* LIZ *sip tea*.

SHEA   I'm a Palace spokesman so obviously I'm not
           going to speak
           I have no comment
           And Her Majesty is not at liberty to say
           But Mrs Thatcher's style was becoming very regal
           She began to use the royal 'we'

MAGS   I am not an 'I did this' 'I did that' person. I have
           never been an 'I' person. I prefer to talk about

	'we' – the Government… it is not I who do things, it is we, the Government
T	We have become a grandmother
LIZ	One can't help feeling one is being copied
SHEA	Her Majesty never said that
MAGS	Ma'am, may I ask what colour you'll be wearing to the
LIZ	One never notices what one is wearing

Another teatime over.

T	Wets
MAGS	Do you know what a 'wet' is?
T	My backbench was full of them
MAGS	Wets and ultra-wets
T	They were the remnants of public school, Victorian philanthropy
LIZ	Great builders of hospitals and schools The British Library Didn't they do that?
MAGS	To be wet is to be like a soggy August The whole concept reminded me of / Balmoral
T	Balmoral
Q	I'm sorry to tell you that the Prime Minister didn't much enjoy Balmoral
T	Having to wear wellingtons Torment I'd never owned a pair in my life
Q	She came for three days every year like all my PMs. Harold Wilson always brought his dogs They had a very jolly time
MAGS	Picnics

Q	I know our life up there does not appeal to everyone But it is home And when one opens it to guests
T	A piper walking round the table after dinner
LIZ	She used to leave at six in the morning Really as soon as she could One found it rude
Q	Hurtful
MAGS	Our Monarch I'm sorry to tell you Is wet
Q	One wondered if she was a religious person
LIZ	No one didn't
Q	Yes one did. One talked about it with Dr Runcie
LIZ	Oh yes
Q	He felt sure that the Prime Minister believed, But he wasn't sure that the doctrine of grace meant much to her
SHEA	Does anyone remember 1986? It was quite a bumpy year for me
Q	I expect a lot of you were not yet born Or still at school Or listening to all those dreadful bands Diana used to like
SHEA	I'm the Queen's Press Secretary I have a background in diplomacy And I also write thrillers under a pseudonym Pretty good ones in fact. Wipe the floor with Jeffrey Archer's. I didn't say or do anything that you're about to hear

Q   Of course he didn't
             It's offensive ill-researched conjecture

LIZ   In 1986

SHEA   After the miners' strike
             And the race riots
             As unemployment reached four million
             After an Irish terrorist had been elected to our
                  Parliament
             And starved himself to death
             After we'd allowed America to send bombs to
                  Libya from our shores

RON }   That was the right decision
MAGS }   That was the right decision

SHEA   The international community was putting pressure
                  on Great Britain
             To impose sanctions on South Africa

LIZ   I had visited it with my parents when I was a girl
             Fond memories of wonderful people
             Lots of big game

T   My son Mark was working there in finance at the
                  time
             So I knew a lot about the situation
             Dennis had a lot of colleagues there

MAGS   Anyone who thinks the ANC can form a
                  government is living in cloud-cuckoo-land

Q   Apartheid
             Now, we fought against the Nazis
             And I could see no difference

SHEA   Actually she didn't say that

LIZ   The Commonwealth cannot support apartheid
             We favour sanctions

             More tea.

MAGS   To impose sanctions on South Africa
Would be inimical to British trade

RON   And American trade
Margaret and I, yet again we shared a vision
You know, I attempted to veto US sanctions but
can you believe it?
I was overridden by Congress

T   I had Ron's personal support if not his
Government's

RON   First time this century that any president was
overruled on foreign policy

T   Why did they not see that he was right?

RON   Margaret, we were just too far ahead sometimes

T   Oh, Ronnie

LIZ   Would you like a scone, Prime Minister?

MAGS   Thank you, ma'am

LIZ   The jam is home-made this week
There's damson and that one's bilberry

Q   I didn't say that
We never have bilberry jam
I'm not even sure if it exists

LIZ   One likes to support the village fêtes around
Sandringham
One's always buying little jars at local sales of
work

MAGS   I think one's always looking for the jam that tastes
like home. No one made jam like my mother
could. She was very much a woman of the
home and I can remember the smell of her
gooseberry like it was yesterday

LIZ   Yes, my sister and I made jam, too

MAGS	I don't think there's a woman of our whole generation who can't make jam
LIZ	And marmalade
MAGS	We all learnt from the homily of housekeeping And I still believe it would save many a financier from failure
LIZ	I couldn't agree with you more
Q	You see, sometimes it was nice
LIZ	But this question of sanctions for South Africa –
MAGS	Ma'am, you understand our policy
LIZ	But one has an opinion
MAGS	A private opinion, ma'am
LIZ	A very well-informed opinion The Commonwealth is unanimous in thinking that sanctions
MAGS	Sanctions would be ineffective They'd plunge the poor into further poverty –
Q	She went on to –
MAGS	Sanctions are immoral Sanctions are repugnant
LIZ	But one sees people seeking basic human rights Being violently suppressed – Surely this is the very thing That you abhor in Communist countries This utter lack of freedom And this brutal state control?
MAGS	The political science here, ma'am Is quite different
Q	Patronising
LIZ	There comes a time, Prime Minister,

When morally
One must say no

MAGS   I thank you very kindly for your point of view
And for your wise advice

LIZ   We must say no to this apartheid

MAGS   I have enjoyed my scone
The jam was quite delicious

Tea over.

SHEA   The Queen was in a serious predicament
As leader of the Commonwealth her role was clear
To universally support the sanctions
But as Monarch
She was not allowed to.
She felt, however

LIZ   I felt

SHEA   That to say nothing
Would be to implicitly support the Government
And give credence to a policy she privately
    abhorred
It was intolerable

LIZ   Michael, how can you presume to know how I
    was feeling?

SHEA   I didn't, ma'am
I've never said a word about it

Q   This is impertinent, insulting paraphrase

T   I began to feel that anything the Commonwealth
    preferred
Demanded opposition

MAGS   It was a multi-racial quango

Q   Don't hold back

T   Dominated by the Third World

MAGS   I never said that
            There's no record that I thought it

Q   But you did
            And your attitude trickled down
            You were tearing the Commonwealth apart
            And in my Coronation speech
            I had vowed to serve it

SHEA   On July the 20th the *Sunday Times*
            Announced Her Majesty's dismay
            At the policies of the Government

T   A huge, huge spread

SHEA   A dismay which went far beyond the issue of
                sanctions

T   Pages

SHEA   The journalists
            Michael Jones, highly respected political editor
            And Simon Freeman (backstabbing bastard)
            Claimed irrefutable evidence
            That the Queen found her Prime Minister

MAGS   Uncaring, confrontational and socially divisive

SHEA   It was very precise

T   The journalists said the Queen was fully aware
                that it would be published

SHEA   Here are the bullet points: One –

Q   One feared that the suppression of the miners'
                strike had done long-term damage to the
                fabric of the state

SHEA   Two –

Q   One objected to America's bombing raids on
                Libya departing from British airbases

SHEA   Three –

Q	One supported sanctions in South Africa and abhorred apartheid
SHEA	Four –
Q	One had deep concerns about our own disintegrating race relations and inner-city decay
SHEA	And that overall
Q	One felt the whole direction of Government policy was –
T	What a betrayal
Q	Never said it Never wrote it Nothing to do with me
MAGS	Ultra-wet Ultra-ultra SDP Liberal Alliance wet
T	For an unelected Monarch To oppose the Government – Unconstitutional and dangerous
Q	One is moderate, of course, in all things
SHEA	Ironically we were together when the news broke
T	No we weren't
SHEA	One of the rare occasions I was with them both The Queen Lady Thatcher and myself Up at Holyrood It was breakfast time And the papers were out

MAGS *and* LIZ *are both reading the revelations.*

Well, I couldn't eat a thing
The silence was so sickening

The loudest silence I have ever heard
As if inside their minds were
Whirring and computing and dissecting
The Queen ate scrambled egg with toast
Lady Thatcher sipped her drink.
She had a lot of make-up on that day
Her face was quite unmoving

LIZ   Well, one wonders how this happened, Michael

SHEA   I'd like to apologise
Profusely to you both
Your Majesty
Lady Thatcher
I'm so very, very
Yes, it's true, I did meet Simon Freeman
And we were talking off the record
Quite informally
About an article that he was planning
In the future
And he asked about the Commonwealth

I replied that as Head of the Commonwealth
The Queen...
Is naturally very keen on it
And so forth
The rest is all his supposition
They have put a slant on it
On everything I said
That I would never have intended
Prime Minister, I can assure you that
I had no briefing with Her Majesty.

MAGS   Is that the truth?

T   I never asked that question

Q   And I never answered it

SHEA   The Queen had no prior knowledge of this article
And indeed
I have never, ever heard her

Speaking critically of you
Or any of her previous Prime Ministers

The silence continues.

Mrs Thatcher said only three words to me:

MAGS   Never mind, dear

SHEA   That was it

T   Never mind, dear

SHEA   And I left them
Six months later I resigned

He bows. He leaves.

T   I was knocked sideways
I was very, very down

LIZ   Margaret

T   Her remarks had isolated me

LIZ   Margaret, I am very sorry this has happened

MAGS   Thank you, ma'am

She sips her drink.

Really, I am so respectful

LIZ   That is mutual, you know

Tea over.

Q   There was never any rift

T   Of course not

Q   There was no collision

T   Ever

MAGS   We passed sanctions some time later, and of
course the rest is history

Q   Mrs Thatcher won the next election with a huge
majority

| T | And the Commonwealth
Though shaken
Still endures |

Q   It could have really changed the world

T   One's work is one's legacy

Q   And one's children

LIZ   Yes, one's children

MAGS   One's children can be

LIZ   Yes, they can indeed

Q   By 1990, Lady Thatcher seemed increasingly alone

T   Although I admired George Bush
I missed the intimacy I had shared with Ron

Q   In our constitution, which I so admire
The monarch has no power
But I watch power
I've spent a lifetime in the ebb and flow of it
It brings its gifts
But then it's an intoxicant

LIZ   One must beware lest one consumes too much

MAGS   I pushed through an increase in the civil list,
giving Her Majesty a big pay rise well above
the level of inflation.

LIZ   She said that

MAGS   We regard the Royal Family as the greatest asset
Britain has
They are a focus of patriotism, of loyalty, affection
and of esteem. That is a rare combination and
we should value it highly

LIZ   Hmm

MAGS   There comes a day, of course
When all Prime Ministers relinquish power

Q   For me that day will only come with death

MAGS   The men
           All turned on me

LIZ   When one sees you in the House
           And hears them baying at you
           One can't imagine how you keep your poise
           They really are so dreadful
           Like an awful pack of schoolboys

MAGS   Yes, they can be odious
           But I thrive on it, you see
           I stand out in my blue and blond
           And thrive
           I've always liked an argument

LIZ   Quite so

MAGS   Without it I'm not sure what I will do

           MAGS *curtsies. She leaves.*

Q   One has been lucky
           I suppose one has been blessed.
           As a human being one always has hope
           And perhaps the gambling instinct too.
           One backs one's horse
           And hopes it will be better than the next man's horse

LIZ   I'm not sure what you mean by that

Q   No

           LIZ *leaves.*

           The Baroness read out the eulogy when Ronald
                Reagan died
           It was impeccable, so heartfelt

T   We here still move in twilight, but we have a
                beacon to guide us. We have his example. Let
                us give thanks for a life that achieved so
                much for all of God's children.

Q   I'd have put it slightly differently I think.
           The fortieth President
           Like Michael Shea, our dear Press Secretary
           Died of dementia

T   One doesn't die of dementia, ma'am
           One lives with it

           They are both standing.

Q   Won't you sit down?

T   No

BLOODY WIMMIN

Lucy Kirkwood

Lucy Kirkwood is under commission to Manhattan Theatre Club and is working with Headlong Theatre. Lucy's play *It Felt Empty When the Heart Went At First But It Is Alright Now* premiered at the Arcola Theatre, London, in 2009, and was nominated for the Evening Standard Most Promising Playwright Award, and the Susan Smith Blackburn Prize. In 2008, Lucy's play *Tinderbox* was produced by the Bush Theatre, and *Hedda*, her adaptation of Ibsen's *Hedda Gabler*, was produced by the Gate Theatre. Lucy is currently developing an original TV series for Kudos and a screenplay for Film4/Ruby Films.

Characters

HELEN
LITTLE GIRL
MARGARET
HANNAH
REPORTER
GRAHAM
LORRAINE
BOB
JACK
LIV
DAN
LOU
JAMES
SOPHIE
LILLIAN

Note on the Text

A forward slash (/) in the text indicates the point at which the next speaker interrupts.

A star (*) before a line indicates simultaneous dialogue.

1984

A clock ticking. Might almost be a Geiger counter.

A wire fence. An angry, sturdy thing, three strands of barbed wire across the top. On the other side of it, an RAF base.

HELEN, *thirties, enters. Visibly pregnant. Six months, say.*

Suddenly, a wall of sound, she looks up as a plane roars over. The missiles are arriving at Greenham.

She clicks on a hand-held Dictaphone.

HELEN. At the hypocenter, everything is vaporised.

> *A LITTLE GIRL enters. She has with her lengths of glittering yarn. She weaves it into the fence, creating large, sparkling spider's webs. She sings as she does, quietly, under* HELEN, *under the ticking:*

LITTLE GIRL. * Go to sleep you weary women,
   Let the squaddies go shouting by,
   Can't you hear those launchers rumbling,
   That's a peace-camp lullaby.
   Don't you worry 'bout the bailiffs,
   Let evictions come and go,
   You're safe tucked up in your nice warm Gore-tex,
   Far away from the ice and rain and snow.

HELEN. * Moving outwards, the casualties are caused by
   burns, by falling debris, by the effects of radiation sickness.
   The radioactive particles enter the water supply. They are
   inhaled and ingested. Effects of radiation poisoning include:
   hair loss, destruction of the thyroid gland, reduction of the
   blood's lymphocyte count leading to leukaemia and
   lymphoma. Nausea, bloody vomiting and diarrhoea.
   Stillborn children. Malformed children. Sterility.

I am camped close to the perimeter fence tonight, my darlings.

On the other side of this fence, are ninety-six ground-launched US Tomahawk missiles.

Each one has four times the destructive power of the bomb that hit Hiroshima.

HELEN *holds up a pair of bolt cutters.*

I am now holding a pair of American-made, thirty-six-inch bolt cutters.

They like American things here.

She clicks off the Dictaphone and exits.

The LITTLE GIRL *turns, sees us. She smiles.*

Blood seeps from her gums.

The clock stops ticking. She laughs and runs off.

The space is filled with sound and bustling activity, chatter, songs, the crackle of campfires. Woman upon woman enters at speed. Some are men dressed as women. They stick or tie various objects to the fence, photos of children, baby clothes, flowers, tampons, peace slogans, feeding bottles, quicker and quicker they come until the fence is covered. A shopping trolley full of domestic necessities: cooking equipment, plastic sheeting, bowls of food are given out, someone gets a fire going, someone is washing up in a plastic tub, someone else drying. A chaotic, grubby ecosystem.

A female REPORTER *enters. Mid-thirties, a whole punnet of plums in her mouth. She has a cameraman* (GRAHAM) *with her who can either be played, or simply addressed by her but remaining invisible to us. She surveys the camp with delighted disgust.*

REPORTER. God. Dismal. Perfect. Shot of that tent, please, Graham.

MARGARET *enters, firewood in her arms.*

MARGARET. The wood's got damp again. I said, didn't I? /
Am I mad or did I say – (*To* REPORTER.) You alright there?

The REPORTER *smiles cursorily at her, nods, continues.*
Directing GRAHAM.

REPORTER. That one. The plastic nightmare. / Get a close-up
of the mould on the sleeping bag.

MARGARET. Okedoke. Lovely job on the washing up, Helen
– * anyone seen Helen?

HANNAH. Sent her for a nap.

REPORTER. *And I think, don't you, some general estab-
lishing shots of the debris, a general sense of squalor would
be nice. And faces, we must have faces, Graham, no! Not
that one, she's a bit, don't you think? Bit urban. What about
this lady here? In the chunky-knit?

The REPORTER *continues sniffing round. She is regarded*
suspiciously by the women. She scribbles notes and prepares
to address the camera. LORRAINE, *seventies, enters,*
harassed.

LORRAINE. Margaret, sorry, can you play Solomon for a tick?

MARGARET. What's the problem?

LORRAINE. Well, it's the age-old whadyoucallit; Sonia's
saying it was decided she'd be chef *ce soir*, she's all set on
debuting her smoky bean bake, but – crisis – Jan and Jules
say they were promised kitchen duties, they've spent the
whole day foraging and they're, I'm sorry to say, they're
peeved that Sonia seems to, in their words not mine, Margaret, 'rule the effing roost' where the daily operations of
Violet-gate are concerned.

MARGARET. Well, there's an obvious solution here, isn't there –

LORRAINE. Let me stop you right there, Margaret, because I
think I know what you're about to say –

MARGARET. Why / don't they all cook together –

LORRAINE. Why don't they all cook together, exactly, well yes I did present this as an option to the ladies, but Sonia, bless her, reminded me that she's currently working through the traumatic legacy of Keith's abusive behaviour, both in an emotional, physical and sexual sense and as such, in her words again, Margaret, being 'coerced into a threesome' would stir up rather upsetting memories for her – and Jan and Jules, apparently, have trust issues with Sonia following the Trojan Mushroom debacle so –

MARGARET. Sorry, the / Trojan –

LORRAINE. I can't get into it right now but I will say it might be worth reiterating to the women that food allergies are not to be trifled with – ha, ha! So to speak, now, matter in hand, how do you suggest we smooth the waters?

MARGARET. For pity's – just bang their heads together and we'll all go without dinner.

LORRAINE bursts out in hysterical laughter. Stops.

LORRAINE. No but seriously, Sonia has, to all intents and purposes, taken the only operational ladle hostage, which makes things a smidge more / expedient, what's this?

MARGARET has brought out a coin from her pocket and handed it to LORRAINE.

MARGARET. Here.

REPORTER. Okay here, Graham? Okay.

Fluffs her hair a little in the (invisible) monitor and does a final check of her notes.

LORRAINE. Some sort of trust exercise?

MARGARET. No, it's a five-pence piece. Make them flip for it. Heads, tails, whoever wins cooks.

Beat. LORRAINE sucks in her breath.

Lorraine?

LORRAINE. Yeah, no it's just I don't know how comfortable they'll be using a symbol of Capitalist hegemony to negotiate what is at bottom a psychic impasse.

The REPORTER *gives a big sycophantic grin to the women behind her.*

REPORTER. Sorry, ladies, but could you just be a weeny bit quiet for me? Cheers.

*She turns back to us. From here the two sections marked with an * run over each other, with* MARGARET *and* LORRAINE *initially keeping their voices lowered, but then forgetting themselves. The* REPORTER *matches them, struggling to be heard as their volume increases.*

* Ready?

Beat. Then the camera starts rolling.

Scenes of mayhem unfolded yesterday as, more than two years after their first arrival here, peace protesters took to arms for the first time to cut away several miles of the nine-mile perimeter fence around the American base here at RAF Greenham.

After the arrest of one hundred and eighty-seven women, the mood in the camp is calm this afternoon, but with the missile launchers thought to be arriving within days, the question on the women's minds must surely be –

MARGARET. * I'm asking them to flip a coin, not fellate Geoffrey Howe.

LORRAINE. Yes, but people have beliefs, don't they, and you have to respect those beliefs or –

MARGARET. How much more we could achieve if no one had any sodding beliefs!

LORRAINE. Well, that's academic, isn't it, because they do, so what am I supposed to tell them?

MARGARET. Tell them I'm cooking. Tell them I'm going to scrape some hedgehogs off the road and make kebabs.

LORRAINE. I hope you're joking, Margaret, because –

MARGARET. Of course I'm bloody joking!

MARGARET storms away from LORRAINE, *striding across the front of the* REPORTER*'s shot, unintentionally and oblivious.*

REPORTER. OH, WELL DONE, YOU TIT!

MARGARET turns, surprised.

I'm trying to do a piece to camera here!

MARGARET. I only passed through!

REPORTER. Yes, but the ass eds won't use the bloody thing if you're whizzing about in front of me.

MARGARET. Don't be ridiculous, 'whizzing' –

REPORTER. I've asked you to keep it down, politely I asked you, didn't I? Graham, wasn't I polite?

MARGARET. You're not being very polite now.

REPORTER. That's because you just ruined my bloody piece!

HANNAH, eighteen, seated in the background, starts yelling.

HANNAH. No one here cares about your piece!

REPORTER. Did anyone ask you? Silly cow.

MARGARET. There's no need to speak to her like that –

HANNAH. That's it, come on! We know / what side you're on!

REPORTER. Look I'm sorry I lost my rag, / but really.

MARGARET. This is a space of non-aggression. You do not come here and –

REPORTER. All I'm trying to do is put your side across.

HANNAH. You're on the side of suicide, genocide and / homicide!

MARGARET. Yes, thank you, Hannah, calm down please.

REPORTER. And what do I get, I get hostility and non-cooperation. I mean really. Do you think Mrs Thatcher got where she is by frigging about in the mud?

HANNAH. Yeah, but we don't keep our power in our fucking handbags! We're speaking a new language, love, and you don't like it cos you don't understand it!

REPORTER (*making an effort*). Well, alright. Explain it to me then.

MARGARET. If I could step / in here I might be able to –

HANNAH (*singing*). We are women, we are women, we are strong, we are strong, we say no, / we say no, to the bomb…

REPORTER. For pity's sake. (*Singing back, over.*) Oh say can you see! By the dawn's early light! What so proudly we hailed, / by the twilight's first gleaming…

MARGARET. Well now, that's just childish –

HANNAH. YOU'VE HAD A SPIRITUAL LOBOTOMY, LOVE!

MARGARET. HANNAH!

HANNAH. Go on! Fuck off back to hell!

REPORTER. Graham. (*She whistles at him.*) Come on.

The REPORTER *gestures to her cameraman then exits.* HANNAH *runs off after her.*

MARGARET. Well done! Marvellous, / just –

LORRAINE. Margaret…

MARGARET. Bloody marvellous, that's why!

LORRAINE. That's why what?

MARGARET. That's why in December it was 'thirty-five thousand caring mums and grannies embrace the base', and the rest of the time it's 'six thousand angry lesbians'.

LORRAINE. But I am an angry lesbian.

MARGARET. We need a strategy, training maybe. Dealing with the press, we did it with anti-riot.

LORRAINE. We'll put it to a meeting.

MARGARET. But it's not just, I mean, we're here for the long haul, aren't we? So there's all sorts of things we should be – the latrine situation, for example.

LORRAINE. Oh dear, have the dogs been digging it up again?

MARGARET. No, it's just – the way it looks to people.

LORRAINE. Margaret, I'm a seventy-six-year-old life-model. I stopped worrying about the way I look to people a long time ago. The meeting's on Tuesday, you can raise your concerns then.

MARGARET. Go round a circle for six hours, you mean, yes I agree with that, yes I agree with that, yes I agree with that, then someone feels a bit iffy and the whole proposal's / thrown out –

LORRAINE. I know. But it's consensus, it's important / everyone has their say.

MARGARET. Consensus, of course, I agree but –

LORRAINE. If you don't mind me saying, I looked at you just then, I looked at you and what I saw was not Margaret Sinclair – woman, sister, carer, lover, friend. Do you know what I saw? I saw a bottle. A big, Margaret-shaped bottle full of swirling emotions, full of feelings, with a – what's this! – with a cork wedged in tight at the top. Nothing getting out.

Off, a scream. MARGARET *looks toward it.*

MARGARET. Lorraine –

LORRAINE. And what I'm thinking is, how about you and me make ourselves a nice cup of tea and sit by the fire, have a cigarette, whatever, and we just – ee-ee-ee – see if we can't loosen that cork?

MARGARET. My cork is fine, I like my cork, don't touch my cork, please –

HELEN *enters. Still pregnant. Drenched in blood. Dazed.*

LORRAINE. Oh my / godfathers.

MARGARET. What the hell happened to you!

HELEN. I don't –

HANNAH *enters, after* HELEN.

HANNAH. It was the Newbury lot. Her tent's ruined. Maggots everywhere.

HELEN. I'm going home.

MARGARET. Come on, love. We'll wash you down.

HELEN *stands numb in the centre as various women rush round her, bringing towels, wet cloths, clothes, cleaning her up.* LORRAINE *brings her a plate of food.*

HELEN. I'm going home.

LORRAINE. Shh, none of that, please. Here. You'll feel better with something inside you.

HELEN. What is it?

LORRAINE. Curried porridge.

Beat.

HELEN. I'm going home.

The stage clears. The other side of the fence. Two chairs, we are in a kitchen but there's nothing to suggest that. HELEN *sits on one,* BOB *on the other. A long silence.*

BOB. Did you want some tea?

HELEN. Yes. Thanks. But don't – I'll make it.

She makes toward where the tea bags are kept. He rises slightly.

BOB. Sorry, we don't keep them there any more.

HELEN. Oh. (*Beat*.) I've only been gone a couple of / months.

BOB. I just found it more convenient if they were closer to the kettle.

HELEN. Well, that makes sense.

BOB. I think so.

HELEN. Well, that's one good thing to come out of this, isn't it?

BOB. What?

HELEN. Well, you've sorted out the ergonomics of our kitchen.

BOB. Is that a joke?

HELEN. Bob –

BOB. I'm tired, Hell. The girls will be home in a minute and, and and and I'm sorry but I don't have the energy / to, to –

HELEN. I'm sorry.

BOB. You know?

HELEN. Yes. Sorry. How are they? The girls.

BOB *laughs*. HELEN *sits*.

I just want to know.

BOB. Lauren's got herself a boyfriend, the usual, acne, hair gel, he thinks the Lebanon is a pop group but he always brings her home on time. Lizzie cries herself to sleep every night asking for you, but then she's that much younger, isn't she?

HELEN. That's not fair.

BOB. That much more sensitive, you asked me how they / were.

HELEN. Bob –

BOB. You stink. Sorry, that was unkind. But I can smell you from here.

HELEN. They put pig's blood in my tent. It, / lingers –

BOB. Who, the police? / That's criminal –

HELEN. No, not – the locals. They want us out.

BOB. Well, I suppose that's understandable.

HELEN. They say there's a tide of human excrement round the camp.

BOB. I watch you all, you know.

HELEN. It's not true. We're very vigilant about not / polluting the Common.

BOB. On the television and you look ridiculous. I don't mean that in a horrible way. Good people often don't know how to organise themselves very effectively. That's all.

HELEN. It's a process.

BOB. Sure.

HELEN. I wish you could've stayed there with me.

BOB. I expect you do.

HELEN. It's not anti-men.

BOB (*laughs*). Sorry. Sorry but. I woke up –

HELEN. We don't want violence, that's all –

BOB. I woke up surrounded –

HELEN. When the police arrived, we didn't want fights, aggression, / that's why, not –

BOB. Woke up surrounded by, women, *chanting* –

HELEN. I'm not saying it was gone about in the right way / but –

BOB. Actually around my sleeping bag, actually *chanting*.

He closes his eyes, holds his hands out, palms up. Chants, zombie-like.

'Go away. Go away. / Go away.'

HELEN. Bob. Please.

BOB. It might sound funny to you. Personally, I felt like the Wicker Man.

HELEN. You know I was against it, / at first, that's not, but –

BOB. Edward fucking Woodward, what? But then what, but then you decided that you have more of a say in protecting the planet than men, than half the bloody CND?

HELEN. No. But the men talked all night and never did the washing up.

BOB. Bloody feminist ego-trip. / Not cruise, cruise is just a coat-hanger –

HELEN. There're sixteen-year-old girls there, Bob. Would you let Lauren camp out in the middle of nowhere with a lot of young men?

BOB. No, of course / not –

HELEN. Well then.

BOB. Why have you come back?

HELEN. I came back… I came back because.

BOB. Because you know it isn't going to work.

HELEN. No.

BOB *goes to her, puts his arms round her. She leans on him.*

BOB. It's okay. You're allowed. No one will think badly / of you –

HELEN. I'm so tired.

BOB. It's a, you could just look at it like a, well it is, it's a storage facility. It's a preventative measure. It's not like they're taking us to war.

HELEN. In a sense, yes, yes that's exactly –

BOB. Say what you like about Thatcher, she's not just going to follow the Yanks into battle.

HELEN *pulls away.*

HELEN. Since when were you on her side?

BOB. I'm not on her side, you know that, 'on her – ', don't be infantile.

HELEN. I'm not being / infantile, Bob –

BOB. 'Woolly minds in woolly hats,' that's what Heseltine called you, d'you know that? Almost inclined to agree with the wretched bastard.

HELEN. You are.

BOB. Almost.

HELEN. I've only been gone five minutes and suddenly you almost agree with Michael Heseltine.

BOB. Not suddenly, not suddenly, seven weeks actually.

HELEN goes to pick up her rucksack, hung over the back of the chair.

HELEN (*sincere*). I've made a mistake. I'm sorry.

BOB. YOU SAID TO ME (put that down) sorry but, you said a couple of nights, a week tops, I just want to be there, Bob, I just want to register my complaint.

HELEN. I know. And now –

BOB. Seven weeks.

HELEN. I know. And now –

BOB. I think I've been very understanding.

HELEN. You have. You have.

BOB. I just want to know.

HELEN. When I'm coming home.

BOB. Yes.

HELEN. I'm not.

Beat.

I don't. I don't know how to explain it to you. I thought I was coming home.

But I'm not. I thought I was coming home and then I got here and the tea bags weren't where I left them and you weren't either.

I'm sorry. I'm so sorry. I can't.

BOB. So you're just. You're just. Going. / Like that, just –

HELEN. This doesn't feel like my house any more.

BOB. Well, that's because it's not. Sorry to, but technically. If you wanted to, whose name is on the mortgage? Whose name is on the / deeds?

HELEN. I can't help that, can I, I can't can I, just change the law can I, you're allowed a mortgage I'm not, don't be –

BOB. Oh, I'm being? I'm being, I'm the one / being –

HELEN. But if you're talking about money then yes, / yes –

BOB. I am talking about money, money's exactly what I'm talking about, and I can keep the tea bags where I fucking well like. (*Beat.*) Anyway. This is all a bit academic, isn't it. I mean, once the baby comes. Once this blows over. You'll have to, / won't you.

HELEN. There's lots of children / there.

BOB. Have to come home – children maybe, not babies –

HELEN. Yes, babies, lots.

BOB. Not lots, only, maybe, single mothers, okay, if there's no choice –

HELEN. It's a / lovely place.

BOB. If there were lots the council would put a stop to it, I don't think you understand me.

HELEN. One of the other women made a papoose out of a potato sack.

BOB. *My son is not growing up in a potato sack.* I don't mean to – this isn't even a question of – if I weren't your husband, if *this* weren't such a, bloody shambles, I'd still be saying to you, Helen, you cannot do that, you just cannot it's wrong.

Beat.

HELEN. She said she'll lend it me when James comes. The papoose, I'm sorry, Bob, I really feel I have to, well I'm, yes, I'm putting my, you know, putting it down. And I don't mean to be horrible, but I don't really know what you can, sort of... *do* about it.

Beat.

BOB. What are we saying here, are we actually saying that because, James, our child, *our* child yes, James is in your body so you've got the –

HELEN. Yes.

BOB. He's in your body so you've got the.

HELEN. Yes.

BOB. I could call the police. / Get you –

HELEN. It's just until he starts school.

BOB. This is kidnapping, you know that – sorry, till he starts? That's five years away, don't be –

Beat. He realises she's serious.

Is that – five years, Helen?

HELEN (*almost inaudible*). If that's what it takes.

BOB. Sorry?

HELEN. I said if that's what it takes.

(*Soft.*) I'm sorry. What can I do? I'd like to help you. How can I help you?

Pause.

BOB. I'd like to hit you.

Beat.

HELEN. You'd / like to –

BOB. I think it would make me feel better. I'm sorry if that shocks you.

HELEN. No, it's… I'd quite like to hit you too.

BOB. I haven't done anything.

HELEN. No, I know. Queer, isn't it, it's just when you said you wanted to hit me I suddenly thought, I was suddenly, in my head, I was aware that that, that would be –

BOB. Darling.

HELEN. Satisfying. It would be a release.

BOB. I'm not going to hit you.

HELEN (*laughs*). There's only so much non-violence one can take, you know! So much bloody, turning the other cheek. Sometimes you just need to give someone a good smack!

BOB. Just because I said I'd like to, doesn't mean I'm going to. / I would never, ever, you know that, don't you? Helen? I said it so I wouldn't do it. I said it so I wouldn't do it, *Helen –*

HELEN. Sometimes, when I see the police, coming towards my tent, or a soldier, slipping out the fence off to the pub, it takes an enormous, such a huge amount of restraint not to just, walk up and just swing, you know? I punched a girl at school once, it's a lot easier than you think it's going to be, only you don't realise how much it hurts your hand –

BOB. Is it possible you might stop talking about yourself at any point tonight?

Beat.

I'm not going to hit you. If I wanted to hurt you. Which I don't, I have no interest in, that, though you clearly have no such reservations about – me, about hurting me, but if I wanted to hurt you, there are things I could mention –

HELEN *stands and kicks her chair over. A flicker of a hesitation from* BOB, *he continues.*

Things I could remind you of –

HELEN. You said you'd never.

BOB. That would really, wouldn't they, sting, they'd actually leave a mark.

HELEN. Never use that against me you said, never, / a promise.

BOB. I haven't used it.

HELEN. Yes. You have, you brought it up!

BOB. I haven't used / it.

HELEN. You're threatening to –

BOB. Threatening, yes, not using, threatening, I haven't even said the / word –

HELEN. But you've put it in the room.

BOB. Only because you pushed me. Only because the things / you're capable of –

HELEN. There's things I could say to you, you know, you're not Mister, Mister Sheen, clean –

BOB. I never said I was. It's not a competition. / Not a race.

HELEN. I mean, we're both, we both have things, you have, don't you, *things*, do you know what I'm talking about, Bob, do you know what I'm referring to, what thing, specifically?

Beat. They stare at each other.

BOB. Mine is bigger.

HELEN. What.

BOB. I'm sorry but it's true, what I could, / throw at you –

HELEN. Pig. 'Bigger.'

BOB. What I could throw at you is much bigger than anything you could – what're you doing?

HELEN *mimes taking a box out of her bag. She handles the invisible package with care and proceeds to place it between them.*

HELEN. I'm taking it out, Bob.

BOB. It's not even on the same scale –

HELEN. I'm putting it on the table, Bob.

BOB. My firepower is a thousand times anything you / could muster, my darling.

HELEN. You've pushed me to this –

BOB. I only brought it up as a, a, as a – precautionary measure.

HELEN. No not brought up you didn't bring it up you you you you *invoked* it, *exhumed* it more like, if you say it that's / it you know –

BOB. I'm not going to say it. You might say it, but / I'm not going to –

HELEN. I'm not going to say anything / that's not why I came here, so please –

BOB. And I'm not going to say anything either, I'm just saying, it's there if we need it, but we don't, so forget about it, it's a precautionary measure, pretend it's not there.

HELEN. So put it away.

BOB. It's not out.

HELEN. It is, you put it in the room.

BOB. But I didn't say it.

HELEN. It is it's here it's / in the room you –

BOB (*gestures to invisible box*). Put yours away then –

HELEN. No.

BOB. Well then I don't see why I should just, surrender, be /
    shanghaied into –

HELEN. Not until you do, if you do then / I will, this is *mad* –

BOB. Well, I'm not going to. So it's mutual, isn't it, I won't say
    it if you don't and if neither of us say it then everything's
    okay isn't it, / everything's –

HELEN. How did we get here?

BOB. Tickety-boo.

HELEN. You should never have brought it up.

BOB. I didn't say it.

HELEN. No but it's in the room / you brought it up.

BOB. ARE YOU DEAF OR SOMETHING I / DID NOT SAY
    IT.

HELEN. You put it there, yes well maybe I am, maybe I am
    deaf, maybe I'm blind too, I wish I was anyway because then
    at least the next time I find you tongue-deep in the Avon lady
    I won't be able to see the lipstick on your fucking nipples.

    A grandfather clock chimes in, marking six o' clock. Pause.

    I'd forgotten about that clock. I hate that clock. I curse the
    day your father left us that clock.

BOB (*stunned*). You used it. You actually. I wasn't going to –

HELEN (*calm*). It was in the room. You put it in the room. Just
    because you didn't say it doesn't mean it wasn't in the room.

    *She rights the chair, sits, strokes her stomach, hums softly,
    breathes deeply, calmly.*

    I would never have done that to you if you hadn't done it to
    me first.

He stares at her, numb.

BOB. Helen. Helen. Please. Please.

HELEN stares ahead, detached, as BOB cries.

You can move the tea bags back. I don't mind.

HELEN. No. You were right. They're much better where they are.

We should have thought of it years ago.

2009

As Helen and Bob sit there, from off, three clear voices, building like a round:

PROTESTOR ONE (*off*). Oi, Ed Miliband, leave the carbon in the / ground!

PROTESTOR TWO (*off*). Esso, Exxon, BP, Shell, take your war and go to / hell!

PROTSTOR THREE (*off*). Heathrow, BAA, we don't want your third / runway!

The kitchen fills with Greenham Women (some are men dressed as women), as BOB and HELEN remain, growing further apart by the second, the distance between them increasing. Around them, twenty-five years pass; 1984 melts into 2009, and Greenham becomes a London Climate Camp. The women modernise the camp around them, changing their clothes (the men dressed as women reassuming a male gender) and the movements of the PROTESTORS become slick, balletic, choreographed, breathtakingly efficient. Presently HELEN and BOB part and are absorbed into the campers.

The chants of the PROTESTORS *continue under this, blending and building, as other contemporary chants ('Hopenhagen! Hopenhagen!' ,'No new coal!', etc.) are added.*

Finally, the CLIMATE CAMPERS *gather together, we join them mid meeting. A balance of men and women. They use various hand signals to speed the decision making process: a raised hand to indicate they have something to add, a 'T-shape' with one's hands to indicate a technical point about the process of the discussion, silent hand-clapping, i.e. hands raised and fingers waving, to indicate 'I agree', or 'sounds good'. In short, we're seeing here how the consensus model initiated at Greenham has matured and progressed.*

JACK. Okay, the compost loos are now fully operational, it would be great if we could have the solar panels up and running within the hour, now we're here, and the location is public knowledge, everything's going to be happening very quickly. Can I take we take it as read that everyone knows what they're doing?

All silent hand-clap to show their agreement. LIV *raises her hand.*

Liv, you want to say a few words about the kitchen operations?

Quickly, this is a well-oiled process, LIV *nods, steps forward and* JACK *steps back.*

LIV. Okay, the neighbourhood kitchens are all in action now, in the central kitchen I'm going to be running a team system, one team for sauce prep, two on salads, two on cooked meals. As long as the police don't confiscate our cheese graters again we're all set.

Everyone laughs. DAN *raises a hand.*

DAN. Sorry, just while we're on that note, you're all aware that me and the liaison team met with Superintendant Julia Pendry this morning –

Lots of 'Oinks'. DAN *laughs but simmers them down quickly.*

In fact, we had a cup of tea with her! She assures us that the aggressive policing that we saw at Kingsnorth and in the City was something she was keen to avoid. When I pressed her on this she specifically mentioned stop and search, but we haven't got any guarantees, it's possible they'll be using agent provocateurs again so please, let's keep things peaceful, any sign of a ruck, do whatever you can to calm it down. Okay?

Lots of waving fingers. LOU *raises her hand.*

Lou.

LOU. Thanks, just a few things, I'll be manning the press desk today, I'd appreciate any volunteers. There's lots of press about already, obviously any chance you get to speak to them, do, try and get the message across, there'll be a junket tomorrow once the camp is properly up and running but, very exciting but a bit last-minute, *Newsnight* want an interview for tonight's programme, they're setting up in the Well-being tent, I'm going to propose that Sophie takes it, what do we think?

Lots of waving fingers: 'I agree with that.' JAMES, *a white kid, early twenties, makes a 'technical point' sign.*

James? Technical point?

JAMES. Yup. I just wanted to suggest we took a break at this point.

LOU. Is there a reason you want to take a break?

JAMES. I'd like to discuss something with you in private.

LOU. James, this is a consensus process.

JAMES. Okay, but Sophie did the *Guardian*, she did *Women's Hour* –

JACK *makes a 'technical point' sign.*

LOU. Technical point, Jack?

JACK. Yeah, your boobs aren't *quite* big enough for *Women's Hour,* James.

JAMES. That's… very funny, no seriously, hilarious but – I'm just saying, we're supposed to be non-hierarchical, but isn't that compromised if people see the same face every time?

LOU. Sophie's been to court, that's why she's had a lot / of coverage –

JAMES. I've been to court too. No one covered me.

LOU. And Sophie has more media experience.

JAMES. Some hagiography in the *Evening Standard* doesn't count as media experience.

SOPHIE *raises her hand.*

LOU. Sophie –

JAMES. I want to veto.

LOU. A veto means, 'If this decision went ahead I could / not be part of this project – '

JAMES. I know what it means –

LOU. Is that how you feel, James?

JAMES. I just think it'd be, you know, healthier if we all admitted what was / going on here.

LOU. Is that how you feel?

JAMES. No.

LOU. Okay. Do you want to register a minor objection?

Beat.

Sorry, but we're working against the clock here, you can stand aside if you / like –

JAMES. No.

LOU. No? You agree that Sophie is the best person to take the interview?

JAMES *nods*.

You don't want to register a minor objection? You're entitled to if you –

JAMES *shakes his head*.

Okay. Thanks, that's it, folks, keep your phones on, above all be ready, as Dan said, once the police presence properly arrives we'll have to play things by ear.

The group disperses, leaving SOPHIE *and* JAMES *onstage.* SOPHIE *is an attractive mixed-race girl in her early twenties. She starts to make notes on a pad, he lingers awkwardly.*

JAMES. I wasn't trying to be a prick.

SOPHIE. Comes naturally then, does it?

JAMES. But you know why they picked you, don't you?

SOPHIE. Yup.

JAMES. It's a fucking insult.

SOPHIE. Cos I abseiled down a thousand-foot-high power station.

JAMES. No.

SOPHIE. Is it cos I'm doing an MA in Environmental Law?

JAMES. No. It's because you're an incredibly attractive young woman.

Beat.

SOPHIE. If I wasn't fully committed to a policy of non-violence I'd kick you in the bollocks.

JAMES. I know. I'm disgusted too.

SOPHIE. It's incredible.

JAMES. That's what I'm saying.

SOPHIE. You look completely normal, and then you / open your mouth –

JAMES. Hey! I was at Greenham Common when I was a baby. My mum gave birth to me behind a tree –

SOPHIE. Shows.

JAMES. She kept me in a potato sack for a year. Was your mum there?

SOPHIE. Where?

JAMES. Greenham.

SOPHIE. Greenham? Was that something to do with a motorway?

JAMES. You don't – ? Sorry, the Americans? They based a fuckload of nuclear weapons on British soil and…? They were there for twenty years!

She laughs.

SOPHIE. Wow. That's a really long time to achieve, like, nothing.

JAMES. Not nothing, actually, actually not nothing, / you clearly don't –

SOPHIE. Plus, sorry, but seriously, B52s? (*Laughs.*) We're looking at a massive global energy crisis! If any woman's ever drunk enough to mate with you, your kids are gonna be dealing with drought, and crop failures / and –

JAMES. Don't do that.

SOPHIE. What?

JAMES. Don't laugh. It's fucking rude, you don't think there's plenty of people laughing at you right now? When they see you on the telly. When they see your big, Photoshopped portrait in the paper, 'Oh, I ride a bike everywhere', 'Oh, I grow my own quinoa', 'Oh, there are solar panels on my giant forehead' –

SOPHIE. My forehead is not giant.

JAMES. It is, it's abnormally spacious.

SOPHIE. I'm just saying, it's not like they ended the Cold War.

JAMES. Well, maybe / not but –

SOPHIE. I mean, we're not talking Suffragettes are we? They didn't get us the vote or anything.

JAMES. Uh. Sorry. The Suffragettes didn't get you the vote.

SOPHIE. They're about to spend twenty million quid replacing Trident, right?

JAMES. The Suffragettes did not / get you the vote!

SOPHIE. Okay, so why did we get the –

JAMES (*pretending to press a buzzer*). Cartwright, Corpus Christi: The First World War, the role women played therein.

SOPHIE. You never went to Oxford.

JAMES. Nothing in history happens for one reason.

SOPHIE. I dunno why you're getting so upset, / it's not like I –

JAMES. I'm not getting upset but you're saying, maybe I am upset because you are saying, what you're basically saying is Helen, my mum, wasted five years of her life –

SOPHIE. No but –

JAMES. You are, you're saying she might as well not have bothered, she might as well still be married to Bob and not living in some shitty flat in Bermondsey selling home-made birthday cards on the internet when actually you should be thanking her –

SOPHIE. But even if you're right, so what.

JAMES. About what?

SOPHIE. About me doing the interview. Even if the reason is, what you said, cos I'm –

JAMES. Attractive and ethnic.

SOPHIE. And you're a chubby little white boy who apologises for everything he says –

JAMES. Sorry, but that's not true.

SOPHIE. Even if that's why. Well, I'm not sure I care. I'd do a striptease if it got people to listen.

JAMES. Yeah, good idea. Cos strippers often get consulted on environmental policy, don't they?

SOPHIE. You have to play the game, James.

JAMES. They'd probably all be MPs if they didn't have to spend so much time wiping the cum off their bum-cracks.

SOPHIE. You've just got to rise above –

JAMES. Above what? Above page three? Above Moira Stuart getting fired for daring to age? Above every teenage boy in the country watching internet porn and listening to gangsta rap that tells them all women are prostitutes – / why am I having to convince you of this?

SOPHIE. Oh yeah, shit, I hate that stuff.

JAMES. The system's still rotten, it's just rotting more quietly!

SOPHIE. Gangsta rap. Ugh. Nasty little boys with a rhyming dictionary.

JAMES. That's what I'm saying! How can you contend with that?

SOPHIE. I've got a band. We're called The Horticulturalists.

JAMES. The Horticulturalists? As in gardening?

SOPHIE. Yeah. You can listen to our single on MySpace. It's like, feminist hip hop with a sort of breakbeat, kind of seventies kind of Gil Scott Heron, kind of dubby, breakbeaty –

JAMES. Right.

SOPHIE. You should listen to it.

JAMES. I will. It sounds *brilliant*. Does it have a gardening theme?

SOPHIE. Sort of. It's called 'If You Call Me a Hoe I'll Call You a Spade'.

Beat.

JAMES. That's racist.

SOPHIE. That's why it's funny.

JAMES. Fine. You want to engage with a fucking, misogynistic dialectic, go ahead –

SOPHIE. Thanks.

JAMES. No skin off my nose.

SOPHIE. Good.

JAMES. Betray your sex.

SOPHIE. I will.

JAMES. Put on a bloody miniskirt and bend over for the cameras.

SOPHIE. Ay, ay, captain.

JAMES. Don't come crying to me when everyone gives more of a shit about what lipstick you're wearing than what's coming out of your mouth.

SOPHIE. FOR FUCK'S SAKE!

JAMES. What!

SOPHIE. You're doing my head in.

JAMES. And you have a responsibility not to be a sex object on *Newsnight*.

SOPHIE. You're the kind of boy who asks a girl if it's okay to kiss her before he kisses her, aren't you?

JAMES. I don't see how that's, a, that's even I mean what the fuck?

SOPHIE. Yeah well, for your information, *James*, what I look
like and whether I like, wax my fanny or whatever isn't
relevant. It's not a political issue.

JAMES. Yes it is, of course it fucking is – why do you do it?

SOPHIE. Didn't say I did.

JAMES. Do you?

SOPHIE. What?

JAMES. Wax.

SOPHIE. Yup. All of it.

JAMES. All of it?

SOPHIE. Yup.

Beat.

JAMES. Okay. So why d'you do it?

SOPHIE. I do / it cos –

JAMES. You do it because expectation of the male / gaze
creates –

SOPHIE. No, actually –

JAMES. – a fascistic female body image –

SOPHIE. D'you wanna let me speak?

JAMES. – whereby grown women are s'posed to look like
fucking prepubescent / girls –

SOPHIE. No.

JAMES. Because sexual exploitation hasn't gone away, it's just
been repackaged, served up on a girl-power plate when
actually it's the same as it always was and if you don't
present your hairless form for our viewing pleasure you're
dismissed as some sort of man-hating hennaed hippy hemp-
weaving throwback who wants to die alone in a flat full of
cats she calls her babies, and that's why you do it. Right?
Right?

Beat.

SOPHIE. Actually, I do it because it makes my orgasms feel amazing.

Beat.

JAMES. Does it?

SOPHIE. Yeah.

He kisses her. She picks up as if nothing has happened.

See what I mean? Half the stuff that comes out your mouth is just, wrong, / it's –

JAMES. So you agree with the other half?

SOPHIE. What? Yes but –

JAMES. So you agree the other half makes sense?

SOPHIE. Yes, of course I do, I'm not / saying –

JAMES. So which half is it?

SOPHIE. If you don't already know then I don't think I can tell you.

Beat.

JAMES. Right. Well. Good luck. With the interview and, you know, break a leg, etcetera –

SOPHIE. Don't be like that.

JAMES. What? No, it's just – busy. Lots to –

SOPHIE. It's alright. We're on the same side. Whatever happened at Greening Common / is –

JAMES. Greenham.

SOPHIE. Right, well, it's not the sixties any more.

JAMES. Eighties.

SOPHIE. You know?

JAMES. You should really ask someone about this.

SOPHIE. We're on the same side. We're friends, yeah? Yeah?

JAMES. We're friends. Sorry.

SOPHIE. But just cos your mum breastfed you through a potato sack till you were ten doesn't mean you get to tell me what to do, right?

Do you want to come and do this interview with me?

JAMES. Sorry?

SOPHIE. Stop apologising. Paxo's waiting.

Beat. She reaches out for his hand. He looks at her hand.

I've heard he's kind of old school.

I better do most of the talking.

Just don't fuck it up. Okay?

He takes her hand.

JAMES. Okay.

They turn, slip through a gap in the fence and walk together into a barrage of camera flashes. Suddenly the protestors fill the stage again, clearing the camp. We are now back at Greenham but it is still 2009.

LILLIAN enters. She was around fifty in 1983, now around seventy-five. A stick of rock with Home Counties running through her. Beige mac, paisley scarf, good-quality handbag.

SOPHIE sits next to her, her face to the sun, but listening.

LILLIAN. I'd been having the dreams for about six months when I saw the letter.

Nightmares. Babies with twisted limbs, scuttling along the skirting boards, pale boys on the patio trying to get in while something black like a disease fell from the sky, shadows of human fat on the walls of Sainsbury's and bodies buried in the garden.

And of course one watched the television, was aware of this, thing happening, and then I saw the chain letter, your aunt had a copy, I saw it on her desk, Embrace the base, it said. Embrace the base? I said, she said, oh you won't be interested in that, Mum.

But the next morning, I was cooking Ronnie's kidneys for breakfast and I thought about the letter again, and I thought, well, bugger it, Lillian, you're not a revolutionary, but you could help with the washing up.

The morning of the 12th I went into Ronnie's study, and as I was girding the loins I realised I was about to ask his permission –

Are you sure you want to know about all this? It was so long ago.

SOPHIE. We've driven all the way here now, haven't we? Historic Greenham! Go on. Paint the picture. Where was the fence? Here?

LILLIAN. Thereabouts.

SOPHIE. Imagine if I hadn't asked. This would have gone to your grave with you!

LILLIAN. The buzzards aren't circling yet, thank you. So. The morning of the thing, I go into Ron's study and, as I say, as I was girding the loins I realised I was about to ask his permission –

And that in fact I'd never done anything without asking Ronnie's permission. That makes him sound like Robert Mugabe, doesn't it, and he wasn't, he was a perfectly lovely chartered accountant, but I'd never done anything, bought a theatre ticket, or decided how much to put in the postman's Christmas box or painted the dado rails without saying, 'Ron, love, what do you say to this?'

And something in my head said, not this time, Lillian.

It sounds silly, doesn't it, but I've always been a… a man's

woman. I'd look at men, different men, not in a sexy way,
but I'd look at them and think, goodness. Heck. You really
know what's what. You know what you're about.

People like Kenneth Clarke. Or Tom Selleck.

But I never really *admired* women.

And this lot, especially. Saying they were like Suffragettes,
well, that's all very well but –

You look at Mrs Pankhurst in her lovely lopsided hat and her
gorgeous skirts, little nipped-in waist, leg-of-mutton sleeves
and that splendid purple sash, and then the hammer, in her
hand, or the policeman lifting her up, dainty boots dangling
off the ground, and it just sort of takes your breath away,
doesn't it? It takes your breath away, the dignity of it. The
image strikes you and you say to yourself, well, goodness.
Hats off to you, ma'am. And then you think of some grubby
little beanpole with a dyke's mullet, two years of growth at
the armpit and breath that smells like a corpse's bumhole,
tying a Tampax to a wire fence and, well –

The nose wrinkles, doesn't it? I'm not saying it should but it
does. But afterwards. After Greenham…

Beat.

I just think. It's terribly easy to laugh at passion, isn't it?

I arrived about nine thirty in the morning. Wandered for
nearly an hour. Lost. Looking. People had been asked to
bring something, a gift, something that meant something, the
wire was covered. Photographs and babies' booties and
whatnot. Some bossy article in head-to-toe Gore-tex shoves
me towards the fence and tells me in no uncertain terms to
take hands with whatever grubby soul I find there. So I do,
and it's all rather uneventful for a while but soon I pick up a
few chants and the time passes…

And I realise I'm shouting louder. And the words are coming
easier, not just songs but things from my tummy, things
springing from my brain I never knew were there, I'm not

one for blue words but suddenly they're slipping off my tongue like I'm some sort of navvy –

And I'm yelling now, I'm yelling, there's mud all over my mac and my brogues are for the bin and this teenage girl, mohair jumper, dyed crew cut – electric blue, if you don't mind – home-made cigarette hanging out her mouth, glottal stops like you wouldn't believe, she smiles at me, she's gripping my hand, we're gripping each other, and now we're screaming, my throat is sore:

TAKE THE TOYS FROM THE BOYS! TAKE THE TOYS FROM THE BOYS! NO MORE WAR!

And I, feel this, *rage* rising in me I feel, sick but it's completely, coherent, for the first time in my life it's as if my thoughts and my, my emotions are sort of, slipping into each other, meeting, and this anger, it's not like the usual sour ball in my stomach that needs stopping, needs five minutes in the lav with some deep breaths and a talking to the mirror, it's not *hysterical*, it's pins and needles, pricking at every cell in my body and it's clear and reasonable and I know this and so I *throw* myself at the fence, want to tear it down, and I don't realise I'm crying until the girl, with the crew cut, she pulls me away and puts her arms round me and says, It's alright. Chill out. You'll make yourself poorly, luv. You're here. You're visible. You're heard.

My daddy said girls with loud voices got sold to the didicois, that's what I think as I make her mohair soggy. She smells of woodsmoke and BO but I find I don't mind.

Got home about one a.m. Ron was waiting in the kitchen. Odd look on his face. I said, breezy as you like but there's an odd churning in the stomach, I said, You got my note, love? He nodded. He said, I saw you on the television. I said, Did you, he said, Yes.

I said, have you had supper? He shook his head, but of course I already knew he hadn't, the man hadn't so much as glanced at the gas hob the whole time we'd been married, that's just how it was.

So I said, I'm famished, I'll cook us up some eggs, and I'm just making overtures to the omelette pan when he grips hold of my arm, rather firm and says:

No. I'll do it.

I said, what.

He said, I'll cook the eggs. You've had a long day. Sit down. I'll make you a spritzer.

Pause. LILLIAN *beams. Lost in her memory for a moment. Then turns to* SOPHIE.

Look at you. Sunbathing in October.

SOPHIE. You're the one with the patio heaters, Lillian.

LILLIAN. Are we going to do the patio heaters? Again?

SOPHIE. What did you take?

LILLIAN. Beg pardon?

SOPHIE. You said you were asked to bring a gift. To the camp. What did you bring?

Beat.

LILLIAN. Bulbs. Daffodil bulbs, forty of them. Scarlet O'Hara, nice plant. Early flowering. Took a trowel, found a quiet spot away from the fence and stuck them in.

SOPHIE. Flower power! Never thought you'd turn out to be a hippy.

LILLIAN. I wasn't.

SOPHIE. You should come on a march.

LILLIAN. Pfft. With my bunions.

SOPHIE. Like to see them try to kettle you. Did you ever go back?

LILLIAN. No. Not properly. Dropped off a few bags of kindling from time to time but what with me getting the business off the ground and Ronnie's prostrate I had bigger fish to fry.

SOPHIE. Your dreams stopped?

LILLIAN. The moment passed. The fear lifted.

SOPHIE. You should have told me about this before.

LILLIAN. You never asked.

SOPHIE. But you should have told me.

LILLIAN. I never really told anyone. Wasn't any of their business. Rang up your aunt the next day, I said, What did you do last night? She said she'd been to see *E.T.* and had I seen all the silly cows on the television, delivering us into the hands of the Russians.

Beat.

Well. You're entitled to your opinion, aren't you?

I just think.

It is, you know.

It is terribly easy to laugh at passion.

Silence. Then behind them, around them, the stage fills with women. They all carry either a lit candle or a torch. This is the only light on stage.

The women look up at the tremendous sound overhead. The roaring of planes going over. The missiles are leaving Greenham. Daffodils fall from the sky.

They extinguish their candles and torches as one. Black.

Somewhere a clock begins to tick again.

End.